the HOME COMING

Unconditional Love:
Finding Your Place
in the Father's Heart

*How great is the love
the Father has lavished
on us, that we should
be called children of God!*
1 John 3:1a

the HOME COMING

Unconditional Love:
Finding Your Place
in the Father's Heart

JACK WINTER
with Pamela Ferris

PUBLISHING
A Ministry Of Youth With A Mission
P.O. Box 55787, Seattle, WA 98155

YWAM Publishing is the publishing ministry of Youth With A Mission. Youth With A Mission (YWAM) is an international missionary organization of Christians from many denominations dedicated to presenting Jesus Christ to this generation. To this end, YWAM has focused its efforts in three main areas:
1) Training and equipping believers for their part in fulfilling the Great Commission (Matthew 28:19). 2) Personal evangelism. 3) Mercy ministry (medical and relief work).
For a free catalog of books and materials write or call:
YWAM Publishing
P.O. Box 55787, Seattle, WA 98155
(425) 771-1153 or (800) 922-2143
e-mail address: 75701.2772 @ compuserve.com

All Scripture quotations, unless otherwise noted, are taken from the HOLY BIBLE, NEW INTERNATIONAL VERSION. Copyright © 1973, 1978, 1984 International Bible Society. Used by permission of Zondervan Bible Publishers.
Scripture quotations noted TLB are from THE LIVING BIBLE. Copyright © 1971 by Tyndale House Publishers, Wheaton, Illinois. Used by permission.
Scripture quotations noted AMP are from THE AMPLIFIED BIBLE, Old Testament Copyright © 1965, 1987 by The Zondervan Corporation. The Amplified New Testament Copyright © 1958, 1987 by The Lockman Foundation. Used by permission.
Scripture quotations noted KJV are from The Holy Bible, KING JAMES VERSION.

The Homecoming
ISBN 1-57658-004-0
Copyright © 1997 by John H. Winter

Names and certain details used in illustrations have been changed to protect the privacy of the individuals.

Printed in the United States of America.

*Dedicated to the believers in Christ,
across the nations, who have been willing to
humble themselves, become as little children,
and receive the love of the Father.*

Special Thanks

To Dorothy, my excellent wife, who has released me to minister the Father's love to others, and has stood with me when I have struggled.

To Loren Cunningham, who has released me to bring the Father's love to the nations, especially Europe and Asia.

To Fred and Janice Hodgson and Tom Hallas, whom God has used to release me to bring Father's healing love to Australia.

To David and Ellen Ross, who have opened a wide and effectual door to bring Father's love to South Korea.

To David de Carvalho, who has opened the door to Chile, Brazil and Venezuela.

To John and Carol Arnott, who opened up their hearts and church, Toronto Airport Christian Fellowship, to the revelation of the Father's love, which has become the foundation of a great renewal that is touching thousands of people around the world.

To George Glover, who has me back year after year to impart Father's great love to the students and staff at Teen Challenge.

To many others in many nations who have invited us, prayed for us, and released us to share the Father's love.

To all the intercessors who have carried me.

To all those who have shared their stories.

To my friend, Pam Ferris, who spent countless hours planning and formatting this book. Our discussions have been challenging and insightful. You have been more than a ghostwriter. Your revelations and inspiration have made you a Holy Ghost writer.

Table of Contents

Foreword

The story of the prodigal son is my favorite story, and Jack Winter has made it even more pleasurable for me. Jack brings out the rich nuances that Jesus must have had in mind as He told this story so many years ago.

In fact, it should not be called "the prodigal son." This is a story about a father's love, a father so patient and kind that he is unlike any other father on earth. We should call it the parable of the waiting father, for in this tale of two sons and their forgiving father, Jesus explores the themes of conflict, pain, fear, and failure. He opens up to us the depths of sin we are capable of, and the heights of forgiveness He gives to us. He portrays human pathos and religious elitism—all in the same family!

As one pundit remarked, "Thank God the older brother was not the one waiting at the end of the road..." How true. When we fail we need a homecoming to heal us, not a trial to judge us. We need a father to comfort and restore us, not a self-righteous Pharisee to condemn us.

True, we must leave the pig pin. There is no hope in sin, but when we "come to ourselves," as the younger brother finally did, then we want to leave the pig pen. Especially when we know our father waits for us to come home.

Homecoming. Jack Winter shows the way home. It is evident from this book that Jack knows the way home. Let him show you the way...to a homecoming.

Floyd McClung

Part I:
❧ Introduction ❧

"*I Wuv Oo!*"

Following a seminar in Ontario, a woman shared this powerful testimony concerning a baby's need for love:

"Down through the years my husband and I have been foster parents to ten children. To touch these little ones with the love of Christ has been a life-changing experience. But as we look back, one little guy in particular stands out.

"Stephen had been born into a very troubled family that had wanted a baby girl. In fact, the parents had told the brother and sister that should the baby be a boy instead of a girl, they were to have nothing to do with 'it.'

"So, fed with a propped-up bottle, Stephen was rarely held or spoken to, spending most of his time lying flat on his back in his tiny wooden crib. As he grew, bottles of lukewarm milk and fruit juice were placed at the end of his bed for him to pick up and feed himself at mealtimes or whenever he was hungry.

"When the authorities became aware of the situation, all three of the children were removed from the home and placed in foster care. It was decided that Stephen, now 13 months old, would be placed in a home separate from his siblings because of the original rejection.

"When my husband and I went to meet Stephen for the very first time, our hearts went out to this little one. A chubby ball, his eyes were big and brown, but seemingly unresponsive. His head, which was totally out of proportion to the rest of his body, was flat on the back.

"Stephen was unable to sit up, even when assisted. Having gone for over a year with so little stimulation, he seemed locked into a world of his own, oblivious to the sounds and movements around him.

"Stephen had been tested for infantile autism and epilepsy. He had also undergone an EEG. We were told that he would not develop much beyond a small child in terms of overall mentality and that he would demand a lot of our time. Were we willing, were we able, to take on such a challenge?

"Why, yes! Of course. There had never been any question in our minds. From that very first moment in the nursery we had known that Stephen was coming home with us!

"Everything took time. But as we poured ourselves into this little guy, he soaked up all the love his heart could hold. Each day my husband and I could see some evidence of change.

"At first Stephen would not cuddle and resisted any effort on my part to hold him close. Then, as he began to bond with us and trust that we would care for him, he slowly gained control over his body and the world around him. From lying on the floor to being propped up beside my husband, he began to pull himself up and crawl. Now he not only noticed objects that were placed in front of him, but he also began to propel himself across the floor on all fours to retrieve a lost truck or a favorite teddy bear.

"Stephen's first words, which he had heard us say over and over again, were 'I wuv oo.' What an encouragement for the hearts of a mom and dad who had trusted God for a miracle!

"For years my husband and I had been unable to have a child of our own, so Stephen was an answer to prayer. I had wanted a little boy with big brown eyes, and God, knowing the desire of my heart, had delivered!

"About nine months after Stephen was placed in our home, the social worker came to visit. Shocked by what she saw, she could not believe that this was the same little guy that had been so unresponsive in the nursery. He was delightful—full of life and running all over the place!

"'How did you do it?' she asked. 'What brought about these changes?'

"'We talked to him,' I said. 'We sang with him. We prayed for him. We just loved him!'

"A straight 'A' student, Stephen is now in high school. He plays the trombone and loves computers. When he completes his schooling, he wants to serve the Lord as a missionary in Africa."

Inside each of us is a little child that needs to be loved. When we humble ourselves and admit that truth, then and only then can the Father come and minister His love to us.

Chapter One

As a Little Child

He called a little child and had him stand among them. And he said: "I tell you the truth, unless you change and become like little children, you will never enter the kingdom of heaven. Therefore, whoever humbles himself like this child is the greatest in the kingdom of heaven."

Matthew 18:2-4

It was a cool morning in late September. The leaves, which had been slowly turning from deep green to crimson red, yellow, and burnt orange, had just begun to fill the parking lot of this suburban, evangelical church.

It was the beginning of another term, and I had been asked by the leaders of the church to speak to the Sunday school before the classes were dismissed for the morning worship service. As I was facing this large group of children in an open auditorium, I could see in the background some of the parents and teachers, anxiously waiting to hear what I was about to say.

"How many of you want to be 'big' like your parents?" I asked the children. Every hand shot up. I smiled.

"That's really too bad," I said, "because Jesus wants all of these adults who are standing here to change and become little children just like you!"

No doubt the adults in that auditorium were as surprised by my reply as were the disciples that day in Capernaum. For hours the disciples had been arguing, trying to determine who from among their ranks would be selected as "the greatest"—the ones most deserving to sit at Jesus' right and left hand when He set up His kingdom on earth.

Then Jesus calls a little child to come and stand among them and says, *"Whoever humbles himself like this child is the greatest in the kingdom of heaven"* (v. 4).

For some of us this may seem like a contradiction when we reflect on the words of the Apostle Paul:

> *We have much to say about this, but it is hard to explain because you are slow to learn. In fact, though by this time you ought to be teachers, you need someone to teach you the elementary truths of God's word all over again. You need milk, not solid food! Anyone who lives on milk, being still an infant, is not acquainted with the teaching about righteousness. But solid food is for the mature, who by constant use have trained themselves to distinguish good from evil.*
>
> Hebrews 5:11-14

How can we as born-again Christians become mature in Christ, while at the same time becoming *"like little children"?*

The key is in context. Jesus is telling us in Matthew 18:2-4 to become "childlike" in our faith, while Paul is telling us not to be "childish" or immature in our understanding of the Scriptures and our outward behavior.

What distinguishes a small child from a mature adult? How would we describe a boy or girl of four or five years of age?

A child trusts. In simple faith he comes, reaches out his hand, asks, and expects to receive! He does not question his father's willingness nor his father's ability to love, provide, and care for him.

A child is carefree. He does not worry, nor does he try to reason things out. He realizes his limitations, knows he is dependent, and expects to be told what to do.

A child is sincere. Without sham or pretense, he has not yet come to understand the adult art of compromise or the cutting edge of cynicism. He is literal in terms of his interpretation of the spoken word and will take whatever is said to him by others totally at face value.

A child is honest—in fact, blatantly so. With absolutely no warning, he will blurt out the most startling revelation, causing others to smile or blush, depending on what was said and who is present. In his world, truth is not only a pursuit, it is a given.

A child is innocent. With no room in his small world for pain, disappointment, failure, or calculated evil, he will always expect the best from life and those who lovingly care for him.

As we advance in years, most of us will mature both socially and intellectually. With classroom instruction and a variety of after-school activities, our entire educational system is structured and geared to bring this about. But unless we receive the parenting we so desperately need, either as a child or later as an adult, far too many of us will remain emotionally immature, unable to adequately cope with the demands that life will place upon us, both at work and at home.

Hurtful experiences from childhood will continue to haunt us, leaving us vulnerable to feelings of fear, anger, inadequacy, loneliness, and despair. We will struggle to survive, though in every other way—intellectual capacity, natural ability, and personal drive—we will know that inherently we have what is needed to succeed and to advance in our highly competitive world.

Now let's be honest. Let's ask ourselves: As adults are we able to handle the pressures of life? Do we balk when friends, family, and employers offer us a word of advice or correction? Can we set priorities so there is time for family, as well as work and play?

Are we able to love and to be loved? Or are we learning from firsthand experience that the type of sexual intimacy the media exploits is not meeting our need to be held, understood, and valued? With our emotional tanks almost on "empty" are we going in search of something else—drugs, pornography, alcohol, food, or an illicit affair—to meet our desperate need for love?

The simple truth is that we need a father. We need to be parented. That is why, as Jesus shares in this passage from the Gospel of Matthew, we must humble ourselves and become *"like little children"* (v. 3).

One day I asked, "Lord, how can a grown man become like a little child?"

And this was His reply: "Men are just little boys, and women are just little girls, who have gotten big."

Inside each of us is a little child that needs to be loved. When we humble ourselves and admit that truth, then and only then can the Father come and minister His love to us.

Loren Cunningham, founder of Youth With A Mission, once said, "Humility is the willingness to be known for who we really are."

Who are we? We are a people of great need. God has created us, knowing that there will be a place in our lives and our hearts that only He can fill. When we ignore this truth and try to meet that need in any other way, we are simply spinning our wheels and setting ourselves up to fail.

Only a child has the simple faith to reach out and accept what is given to him as a gift. As adults we are too self-sufficient, too achievement-oriented. The first thing we ask when something is offered to us is, "How much does it cost? What do I have to do?"

A child not only holds out his hand and takes what is offered, without question, but he also asks for more!

It says in 1 John 4:19: *"We love because he first loved us."*

We love because HE FIRST loved us. There's a way in which we must experience the love of the Father BEFORE we can know how to love ourselves and others.

This book is a journey, a way for you to experience again that simple faith you had as a child, before life came with all of its pain, disappointments, and fear to betray your trust in a loving and a compassionate Father.

Before each chapter there are stories of people who humbled themselves, became as little children, and received the healing they needed to become loving men and women of God. From all walks of life, with all kinds of problems, they, too, were looking for someone or something to fill that void in their lives that nothing else could fill.

Then sandwiched in between these personal testimonies is the story of a family scandal that is recorded in the Gospel of Luke. Better known as "The Prodigal Son," it is about relationship—or more accurately, the lack of it.

One day God spoke to me and said, "Rather than a big boy with a little Father, be a little boy with a big Father!"

I am convinced that in the Kingdom of Heaven greatness is not dependent upon natural talent, personality, or even intelligence. Greatness is dependent upon our ability to receive and appropriate all that the Father has for us as His sons and daughters through Jesus Christ.

Only a child needs a Father. Can we humble ourselves and become as a little child?

Part II:
❧ The Younger Son ☙

A Rebel Comes Home

"When I was growing up," said Jeff, "I felt that religion was being crammed down my throat. Every Sunday afternoon my parents would have a meeting in our home, invite some spiritual 'heavy' to speak, and force me to attend. I began to resent it.

"We had gone to church in the morning. That was enough. I wanted to spend Sunday afternoon with my friends, playing ball or just hangin' around.

"As I grew older, I became more and more rebellious. I began to hate my parents and openly display my anger towards them.

"My older brother, Jonathan, who seemed to enjoy the meetings, was my rival. Always on my case, he'd confront me with my godless behavior and stinkin' attitude. I hated him, and at best he only tolerated me.

"In seventh grade I began to push drugs—marijuana, heroin, and a variety of 'uppers'—as an act of defiance against my family and against my church. I enjoyed the challenge of selling with the inherent risk of getting caught, as well as the extra bucks my position provided.

"Then in high school, looking for the temporary thrills that my friends were experiencing as they 'popped' pills and shot up with heroin, I, too, began to mainline, devoting more and more of my profits as a pusher to my ever-growing habit.

"After that life went downhill at breakneck speed. Soon the drugs weren't giving me the 'highs' that I needed to get through the day, and I began to look to the occult for answers.

"A friend of mine invited me to a seance, and within a few months I was initiated into a satanic cult. I began to worship the devil, doing whatever he demanded of me. Satanic ritualism, drugs, animal sacrifice, sexual immorality, blasphemy—you name it, I not only did it, but I also encouraged others to join me.

"All along my parents and their friends were praying for me, though they had no idea what I was into. That bugged me and put me under a lot of pressure, but I didn't let it stop me.

"Jonathan, my older brother, who as far as I could tell had never done anything wrong in his entire life, was a constant source of irritation. With a condemning, self-righteous attitude he would roll his eyes and say, 'I wonder what little Jeffie is into now?' Then, goaded into action, I would respond, telling him in no uncertain terms where to go.

"My parents loved me, even when I seemingly did everything they told me not to do, which was most of the time. But as parents, they had rules and expectations. So did my church. From the very beginning it was a losing battle. Anyone could see that I was not cut out to be the model son or the faithful church member.

"Finally I'd had enough. I wanted to live my own life, make my own decisions, and choose my own friends. So I packed my bags and left.

"No one in my family seemed to understand, especially Dad. But I knew, even if they didn't, that life had a lot more to offer a young man like myself than what could ever be found in that straitjacket they liked to call a 'Christian home.'

"After I left, things went from bad to worse. Forced to earn enough money to support my immoral lifestyle as well as my habit, I had to push drugs more openly on the street. For the first time in my life I was afraid. I knew that if the cops were ever to raid my apartment or catch me making a sale, I could spend a lot of time in prison, warming a hard bunk in a concrete cell.

"Not long after that my best friend, Leighton, who had been selling and using with me, was unable to pay the suppliers what he owed them and got beat up really bad. For days I hung around the hospital, wondering if my friend was going to live or die.

"All at once my family began to look pretty good to me, even my older brother, Jonathan. Three square meals, a warm bed, a closet full of clean clothes—it had been tough living on the street, fending for myself. Perhaps I could move back home. Perhaps I could even get some help to kick this habit before it put me behind bars or, even worse, ended my life.

"It wasn't an easy decision. I went through a lot of mental hassle, telling myself I should stick it out rather than go home and admit defeat. Pride was the biggest issue. A man doesn't like to admit he's wrong even if he is. You can understand that.

"But finally I had to face the facts. Life on the street was a one-way ticket to a metal coffin. So I said, 'To hell with it,' packed my bags, and headed home, sweatin' all the way.

"Would you believe—my parents welcomed me with open arms! After all I had done, they were genuinely glad to have me around. They didn't even press me for the details of my lurid past, though my arms and legs were covered with puncture wounds and multicolored bruises where the dirty needles had missed their mark.

"Now don't get me wrong. It wasn't easy. I was still under a lot of pressure as they continued to pray for me, asking the Lord to get ahold of my life. But it was worth it. I knew I was in a safe place and I knew I was loved.

"For years I had mocked God and everything that was even remotely related to Christianity. Now as a two-bit junkie I not only had a habit to kick, but I found myself morally unclean, defiled before a Holy God. My conscience began to torment me, and I was filled with shame.

"The drug abuse, the immorality, and the Satan worship had been sheer rebellion against God, and I knew it. The choice had been clearly mine, not His. Would He forgive me?

"In fear I cried out to the Lord. Was it too late for me to break the hold that Satan had on my life? Like Pharaoh, had I said 'no' one time too many? I began to panic.

"'Lord,' I said, 'I want to repent. I want to be forgiven. Please—please help me to break through. My heart is so hard.'

"As family and friends prayed, grace prevailed. Tears of remorse began to flow down my face as I repented and God saved me."

[A few years later Jeff attended one of my seminars on the Father Heart of God. Again he found himself in a place of rebellion.]

"Jack, having been a servant of Satan and a servant of sin, I now want to go all-out for the Lord. That's why I came to your seminar. But as you began to share the Father's love, I suddenly found myself saying, 'No way will I ever let that man pray for me.'"

"Well, Jeff," I said, "you almost had your wish. You are the last one. Even now they are waiting to take me to the airport."

"I wanted to punch you out. I just couldn't understand what was going on inside of me. Now I realize that I have built a lot of walls. I have consciously chosen to cut myself off from those who love me.

"Jack, I want to break through those walls, but I don't know how or where to begin."

"Jeff, God not only wants your life, He wants your heart. He wants to touch all those areas of your life that are still causing you pain and minister His love to you.

"Can you humble yourself? Can you become as a little child? Can you be that little boy that needs a Father?"

"I think I can. No, I will," said Jeff with determination. "I want Him to be my Father."

As we prayed, God met Jeff in a powerful way. It wasn't anything that I said. It never is. It was what God did in his heart that day that brought about the change.

Now Jeff is not only a son who is loved by his Abba [Daddy] Father, but he is also an effective servant who is able to share that love with his family and with others.

It had been a long journey, but like the prodigal, Jeff had come home!

The younger son values his inheritance, but he takes for granted—or perhaps he doesn't understand—the committed love his father has for him. He doesn't value the relationship.

Chapter Two

Leaving Home

*Jesus continued: "There was a man who had two sons. The
younger one said to his father, 'Father, give me my share of the
estate.' So he divided his property between them. Not long after
that, the younger son got together all he had, set off for a distant country and there squandered his wealth in wild living."*

Luke 15:11-13

*J*eff's parents loved him, prayed for him, and desired the very best
for him. But unable to receive that love, Jeff responded in anger,
left home, and became hopelessly enmeshed in a world of drugs, Satan
worship, and sexual immorality.

Most of us, like Jeff and the two sons in Luke's parable, have a history of broken relationships. What we most desire, the unconditional love
described in Paul's epistle to the church at Corinth, more often than not
becomes the source of our greatest pain.

*Love is very patient and kind, never jealous or envious, never
boastful or proud, never haughty or selfish or rude. Love does
not demand its own way. It is not irritable or touchy. It does not
hold grudges and will hardly even notice when others do it
wrong. It is never glad about injustice, but rejoices whenever
truth wins out. If you love someone you will be loyal to him no
matter what the cost. You will always believe in him, always
expect the best of him, and always stand your ground in defend-
ing him...love goes on forever.*

1 Corinthians 13:4-8a, TLB

This is the story of a broken relationship—a young man who is leaving home and a father who is grieving the loss of his son.

Traditionally called "The Prodigal Son," it could just as well have been called "The Prodigal Father," for *prodigal* is a word that means recklessly extravagant, one who gives or spends lavishly. In this story that Jesus relates to the scribes and the Pharisees, the father is as lavish in his love for his younger son as his younger son is recklessly extravagant in his day-to-day spending.

As the story begins, we see two brothers, both of whom have a relationship with their Jewish father through natural birth and the rite of circumcision. The younger son is rebellious and full of passion, while the older son is obedient and emotionally restrained. Both live in their father's house where everything is provided for them, even love which, as we'll see later, neither of them is able to receive.

Now one of the things that is good about this younger son is that he is aware that his father has an inheritance to give him, and he is bold enough to ask for it. What is troublesome or unusual about his request is that he comes to his father, demanding his share of the estate, while his father is still alive. Even under Roman law, which shapes the concept of inheritance in the New Testament, a child comes into his or her inheritance rights at birth, but does not take actual possession until the parent has died.

Though the significance of this request might be lost to those of us who live in a more permissive Western culture, where adolescents often rebel, leave home, and make some foolhardy decisions, to the Jewish people and to those born in the Middle East this request would have been seen for what it is: a radical and extremely offensive departure from tradition.

In anger this young man is saying, "Father, I can't wait for you to die. Give me what is rightfully mine so that I can leave home and get on with life!"

It is an unspeakable act, an insult. No Jewish son would ever think, let alone speak, such a word to his father! If he were to do so, he would most certainly be beaten, and perhaps even disowned.

But to the scribes and the Pharisees, who can hardly believe what they are hearing, even more radical than the son's request is the father's response! In the midst of his humiliation, brokenness, and pain, the father is not only compassionate, but also extremely generous. He allows his younger son's portion of the estate (about one-third) to be sold so that his son can receive the funds forthwith.

Jesus is very matter-of-fact in His parable, leaving a lot to the imagination of the reader. So we can only speculate, based on the personality traits of the brothers, as to what might have brought this relationship to such a tragic end.

But it is a foolish decision, made in anger during a fit of passion. The younger son is leaving home—for good. He is NOT coming back. It is the end of the relationship, the last time that he will ever see his father alive.

Perhaps some of us can identify with this younger son. Free-spirited, strong-willed, and adventurous, he loves life and enjoys a good party. But when he wants to have fun or try something new, his older brother is always there, on his case, reminding him of his need to work hard, be obedient, and follow the rules if he wants to please his father and succeed in life.

It's a tough situation. The legalistic demands that drive his older brother to achieve and challenge others to do the same, frustrate the younger son who, no matter how hard he tries, can never measure up.

There is enmity—a wall of hostility—between them. Spiritually blind, they both are unable to comprehend the freedom that grace and love could bring to their relationships as brothers and as sons.

So the younger brother is leaving home, taking what is his, and venturing out on his own. Turning his back on his father, his legalistic brother, and the Jewish community that has nurtured him from birth, he is setting off for a distant country where he can make his own decisions and live his own life.

But it is an act of rebellion, disobedience, and dishonor. As a Jewish son he is knowingly breaking the fifth of the Ten Commandments that God gave the children of Israel through Moses on Mount Sinai:

Honor your father and your mother, so that you may live long in the land the LORD your God is giving you.

Exodus 20:12

and he is choosing curse over blessing, death over life:

Cursed is the man who dishonors his father or his mother.
Deuteronomy 27:16a

This day I call heaven and earth as witnesses against you that I have set before you life and death, blessings and curses. Now

*choose life, so that you and your children may live and that you
may love the LORD your God, listen to his voice, and hold fast
to him.*

Deuteronomy 30:19-20a

Believing himself to be wise, the younger son becomes a fool. For a
few pieces of silver, he sells his birthright and allows himself to be
deceived by the father of lies, Satan himself.

*As for you, you were dead in your transgressions and sins, in
which you used to live when you followed the ways of this world
and of the ruler of the kingdom of the air, the spirit who is now
at work in those who are disobedient.*

Ephesians 2:1-2

Reluctantly, and in great sorrow, the father grants his younger son's
request. As a father he has tried everything he can think of to dissuade him
from making this rash decision, but to no avail.

The younger son values his inheritance, but he takes for granted—or
perhaps he doesn't understand—the committed love his father has for him.
He doesn't value the relationship.

So the father releases his son to go. He doesn't demand that he stay,
for he knows that a relationship between a father and a son can never be
forced. Yet, overwhelmed with love and compassion, he watches as his
wayward son packs his bags.

The father is not the one who is leaving. He is not the one who is ending the relationship. If only his son knew, if only he could understand the
love he as a father has for him.

But without submission there can be no lasting commitment. The
father knows that to love and to be loved, one must be willing to die to self
and lay down his life for another. In his immaturity all his son can think
of are his own needs, his own desires.

So the next morning, as the sun begins to rise above the horizon, his son
sets off for a distant country, determined to get as far away from home as
his two legs can carry him. In a Jewish community, where the family structure is so highly valued, this, too, is a blatant act of rebellion. Even after
marriage, sons would continue to live in or near their father's house.

Does this young man know where he is going? Does he have a plan
for his life? Or is he just setting off in a fit of anger, willing to accept whatever town or opportunity might appear along the way?

The word *distant* would seem to imply that this younger man is going into foreign territory, a land where perhaps they do not revere or even know the name of the Lord. For a Jewish son steeped in the religious tradition of his elders, this is indeed a serious severing of family ties. Not only is he leaving the love and provision of his father's house, but also he is turning his back on the religious faith that has guided him throughout his life.

Where do we go when we can no longer tolerate the restrictions and limitations that are being placed upon us by our brothers and sisters in Christ? To a distant country?

Perhaps we don't go that far away, but in our hearts we do begin to leave the accountability and the closeness that we could experience in our Father's house. Usually we separate ourselves emotionally before we distance ourselves physically. It's hard to turn our backs and set off on our own.

It seems like a contradiction. But as society is encouraging us to be independent, self-sufficient, and strong, the very nature of the gospel is calling us to dependency on God and loving relationship with others. How do we resolve the conflict?

We struggle and allow others to do the same. As God has designed a butterfly to emerge from a chrysalis, so we, too, must allow ourselves and others the freedom to undergo whatever trials are necessary to achieve Christian maturity. To abort that process, as with the butterfly, is to bring forth death.

Love is measured by the degree to which we are able to set another free.

What happens when the younger son reaches his destination?

> *"He wasted his fortune in reckless and loose [from restraint] living."*
>
> Luke 15:13b, AMP

Suddenly life becomes a party, and this young man finds himself hopelessly entangled in a downward spiral that ultimately leads to humiliation and pain.

"I Wanted to Have It All!"

"I was going through catechism when my Spirit-filled mother said, 'Ken, if you don't really believe what you're studying, don't go through with it.' It was then that I made a commitment to follow Christ.

"Though Jesus gave me His Spirit and the ability to walk with Him, I thought that God wanted me to develop my own abilities rather than draw on His ability. So I found myself becoming easily confused as to which of my ideas were of God, and which of my ideas were of my own making.

"Later, while seeking direction for a vocation, I decided to go into business for myself. Feeling quite certain that this was an idea from the Lord, I devoted almost every waking hour to making my dream come true.

"My main goal was to have the best remodeling business in the entire metro area. I wanted to own the sharpest trucks that money could buy. I wanted my employees to wear classy uniforms while performing the highest quality work of any business in town.

"The key word for me was *quality*. I not only wanted to build a name for myself, I also wanted to have an image of success.

"At first things went well, and each year the business doubled. Then something happened.

"As profits began to decline, financial pressures began to mount. I had assets on paper, but very little cash in hand. With most of my money tied up in equipment, uniforms, and supplies, I could barely make payroll, let alone pay my creditors.

"Instead of seeking the Lord and relying on His strength to work things out, I relied on my own ability and the ability of others to pull me through. I began to spend long hours with my accountant, banker, and attorney. Then, realizing there was no easy solution to my financial dilemma, I began to panic and make some very unwise decisions.

"The bank that had backed me from the very beginning suddenly withdrew my line of credit. Suppliers withheld orders, demanding payment in full.

"All I could do was begin to sell off the equipment, one piece at a time, and lay off some of my employees. But it was too late.

"As things began to slip between my fingers, I cried out to God. Why? Why was all of this happening to me? Hadn't the Lord told me to go into business for myself?

"As Father dealt with me, I began to understand the motivation of my heart. I wanted to have it all! Driven by love of self and love of money, I had missed the key to real success: the love of the Father.

"Now I began to seek the Lord in earnest and He, faithful to His Word, began to show me how I had been deceived.

Before every man there lies a wide and pleasant road that
seems right but ends in death.

Proverbs 14:12, TLB

I had listened to my own voice and not His. I had relied on my own ability and not His ability. I had disobeyed Him.

"Though I did everything I could think of to avoid it, in the end I had to declare bankruptcy. It was a humbling experience to stand before my family, friends, employees, and creditors and admit defeat.

"I had wanted it all! I had wanted to make a name for myself. Now empty-handed, I had nothing to show for all of my effort except a legal judgment that I was bankrupt—unable to pay my debts.

"For years I had been going after the things of the world. Now I realized that Father was after me! He wanted my heart. He wanted my life. He wanted all of me!

"As Father brought me to the end of myself and literally to the end of my resources, He broke through my resistance. I bowed my knee before Him, repented, claimed His forgiveness, and experienced His unconditional love and acceptance for me as His child.

"Now it is no longer Ken living his own life, but Christ living His life through Ken. What a peace, what a joy that has brought to my heart!

"Though my wife and I have gone through a very difficult time, Father is healing us and restoring our marriage. We know that our lives are in His hands and we are truly excited about the future and the plan that He has for us."

"Do I Need to Tell My Wife?"

After attending my session on "Walking in the Light," Paul came forward for personal ministry.

"Jack," he said, "my furniture business requires that I travel for three or four weeks at a time. Alone at night in an empty motel room, it's easy for me to fall into temptation and begin to seek out female companionship. On many of my trips I have been involved with prostitutes.

"That was over a year ago. I haven't done anything like that since I've become a Christian. Do you think I need to tell my wife?"

"Paul," I said, "I'm sure you could get counsel other than what I am about to give you. But I believe that if you and your wife want to experience the intimacy and fellowship that it is possible to have through Jesus Christ, then your marriage must be based on honesty, forgiveness, and the grace of God."

"Jack, I thought you would say that."

"If Jill knows nothing about this, it will be a real shock to her," I said. "Let's pray that God will prepare her heart."

As we prayed, Paul knew that the Father was pleased. He had made the right decision. Now the outcome of that decision would depend on his wife's willingness to forgive.

"Be sensitive to the Spirit," I said. "You'll know when it's time to tell her."

As Paul left the room, there was Jill, standing in the hallway, waiting for him. "So what did you have to talk about?" she asked.

"Oh," he said, "I had some things I needed to confess."

"Like what?" she asked.

"Oh, I'll tell you sometime."

"Tell me now," she said, "I can handle it."

So ten minutes later, Paul told Jill everything. Then she had to come and see me.

"Jill, why do you think Paul told you these things?" I asked. "To hurt you?"

"No," she said. "I have been a Christian for over six years, but I believe that Paul has read the Bible more than I have. He really wants to be right with God."

"Yes," I said, "and he wants to be right with you. Now the burden is on you to forgive. Otherwise the hurt and betrayal you are feeling will turn to bitterness and you will use it as a weapon against him."

We prayed, but Jill was still in shock.

The next morning Jill came to church. "God awakened me at 3:00 A.M. For over an hour He dealt with me about Paul's confession and my unwillingness to forgive. Then I got Paul out of bed, and we talked for almost four hours!

"At 8:00 A.M. we both went into the shower and washed each other. Then we made love. Jack, it was the most wonderful time of lovemaking that we have ever experienced.

"Before Paul told me about his involvement with prostitutes, I always had this feeling that something was wrong, that there was something 'unclean' in our relationship. Now that feeling is gone."

Six months later I met Paul in the airport. "Jack, our marriage is so wonderful—better than either of us could ever have imagined! I'm so glad that you encouraged me to tell Jill the truth. That was such a critical time for us, and Father really met us and healed our relationship."

Whatever we lust after, whatever we desire will ultimately control us unless we submit ourselves to the love of the Father. Only through the Lord Jesus Christ can we receive the grace we need to overcome temptation.

Chapter Three

The Pigpen

After he had spent everything, there was a severe famine in that whole country, and he began to be in need. So he went and hired himself out to a citizen of that country, who sent him to his fields to feed pigs. He longed to fill his stomach with the pods that the pigs were eating, but no one gave him anything.

Luke 15:14-16

*H*ow many of us have tried to find love in inappropriate and unfulfilling ways? How many of us have looked to the world for answers, fallen into sin, and become slaves to our own evil desires?

Perhaps like Paul we have slept with prostitutes. Or like Ken we have gone bankrupt, trying to have it all!

Whatever we lust after, whatever we desire will ultimately control us unless we submit ourselves to the love of the Father. Only through the Lord Jesus Christ can we receive the grace that we need to overcome temptation.

Such is the case with this younger son. Without the closeness and structure his father's house provides, he finds himself captive to his own passions.

Broken relationships lead to moral weakness. Suddenly, instead of being in control, he finds himself controlled—driven to do things that can only bring shame to himself and to his family.

How long does it take for this young man to waste his inheritance? We don't know—perhaps years, perhaps only a matter of months.

What we do know is that when he has spent everything he has and begins to fall behind, there is a severe famine *"in that whole country"* (v. 14) and he begins to be in need. Now all he can do is hire himself out and become dependent upon another, or go back to his own father.

A job feeding swine would not appeal to most of us, but we need to understand what this would mean in terms of the Jewish culture. Pigs, according to Mosaic Law, are considered unclean.

> *"And the pig, though it has a split hoof completely divided,*
> *does not chew the cud; it is unclean for you. You must not eat*
> *their meat or touch their carcasses; they are unclean for you."*
> Leviticus 11:7-8

Jews neither eat the meat, nor raise swine for others to consume the pork. So the repugnance that they feel for this animal may give us some idea of how low this young man has fallen in his own eyes, and in the eyes of those with whom he has partied.

But this is the price we pay for our sin. When we come to the end of our resources and are forced to rely on another to meet our need, we must accept whatever terms or conditions are laid out for us. Often, as is the case with this younger son, the debt may force us to submit to an act of humiliation.

Why doesn't the prodigal pack up his bags and go home? His father loves him. His father is a wealthy man. Why does he hire himself out to a citizen—a man who cares little, if at all, about him and his needs?

The younger son's heart condemns him. He believes his sin is too great for anyone, including his own father, to forgive.

The younger son is driven, controlled by his sinful nature, and knows he is powerless to change.

The younger son's confidence is gone. He no longer believes in himself or his father's ability to love him for who he is.

Diabolos, a Greek word that means "slanderer," is used 34 times in the New Testament and reflects not only Satan's character, but also the strategy he has used against mankind from the beginning of time.

Remember how the serpent lied in the Garden of Eden to draw Eve into sin (Gen. 3:1-5)? Or how Satan twisted the Word of God in the wilderness to tempt the Lord Jesus Christ (Matt. 4:1-11)?

This is what the devil does here. He slanders, or calls into question, the character of the father by filling the younger son's mind full of lies. Then he tries to convince him that his Heavenly Father is punishing him for his sin.

But the Word of God says:

Do not be deceived: God cannot be mocked. A man reaps what
he sows. The one who sows to please his sinful nature, from
that nature will reap destruction; the one who sows to please
the Spirit, from the Spirit will reap eternal life.

Galatians 6:7-8

There are consequences for every act, whether for good or evil. The prodigal, who has been sowing to please his sinful nature, is now reaping what he's sown—destruction!

Satan is not only a liar, but also the "accuser of the brethren." *Katégoros,* a Greek word that means "accuser," refers to judicial procedure or the act of speaking against another before a public tribunal.

For the accuser of our brothers, who accuses them before our
God day and night, has been hurled down. They overcame him
by the blood of the Lamb and by the word of their testimony.

Revelation 12:10b-11a

Like a prosecuting attorney, Satan goes before the throne of God and says, "This young man has sinned and deserves to die!"

How do we overcome these accusations? By the blood of the Lamb and by the word of our testimony!

My dear children, I write this to you so that you will not sin.
But if anybody does sin, we have one who speaks to the Father
in our defense—Jesus Christ, the Righteous One. He is the
atoning sacrifice for our sins, and not only for ours but also for
the sins of the whole world.

1 John 2:1-2

As born-again Christians we have an advocate, the Lord Jesus Christ, who steps forward and pleads our case. He says, "Father, I am the atoning sacrifice. I went to the cross and shed My blood so that they might go free!"

Then the case is closed! The verdict is in.

Therefore, there is now no condemnation for those who are in
Christ Jesus, because through Christ Jesus the law of the Spirit
of life set me free from the law of sin and death.

Romans 8:1-2

But we must understand this truth, or Satan will do everything in his power to convince us, just as he did with this younger son, that we are beyond redemption. Then, when we believe Satan's lies, we, too, will lose our confidence and withdraw in shame. Jesus, when He described the devil said:

> *You belong to your father, the devil, and you want to carry out*
> *your father's desire. He was a murderer from the beginning, not*
> *holding to the truth, for there is no truth in him. When he lies, he*
> *speaks his native language, for he is a liar and the father of lies.*
>
> John 8:44

Satan is a liar. That is his nature. Only the truth of the Word of God can set us free!

> *To the Jews who had believed him, Jesus said, "If you hold to*
> *my teaching, you are really my disciples. Then you will know*
> *the truth, and the truth will set you free."*
>
> John 8:31-32

In this story of the prodigal son, the pigpen is symbolic. Few of us today would feed swine for a living. What determines whether or not we're in the pigpen is our diet. What are we eating?

I have been in ministry long enough to realize that many of us, as born-again Christians, are involved in alcohol, drugs, illicit sex, and pornography. Without the Spirit and the love of the Father to set us free, we are ruled by our sinful nature.

> *For the sinful nature desires what is contrary to the Spirit, and*
> *the Spirit what is contrary to the sinful nature. They are in con-*
> *flict with each other, so that you do not do what you want.*
>
> Galatians 5:17

Why are we into these things? Our hearts are crying out for love. We think, and wrongly so, "This will satisfy. This will meet my need."

Does this young man find what he needs in the pigpen? No. He feeds the pigs BUT HE HIMSELF IS STILL HUNGRY! The carob pods do not fill his stomach, and even when he asks, no one is willing to give him anything better.

What the world has to offer never satisfies and it always carries a price tag. The younger son comes away hungry, needy, and empty-handed. He has to crawl into the mud with the swine—the ultimate act of humiliation for a Jewish son—in order to survive.

> *When he came to his senses, he said, "How many of my father's hired men have food to spare, and here I am starving to death! I will set out and go back to my father and say to him: Father, I have sinned against heaven and against you. I am no longer worthy to be called your son; make me like one of your hired men." So he got up and went to his father.*
>
> Luke 15:17-20a

When this young man comes to his senses and realizes that even the hired men in his father's house have food and enough to spare, he leaves the pigpen and turns his steps toward home.

How many of us have reached that point in our own lives? How many of us are tired of wallowing in the mud?

God wants to take us from that place where we say, "Give me. Give me what is mine!" to "Father, change me. Make me as one of Your hired servants."

Father is the one we've left. So He's the one we have to go back to if we want to be forgiven, healed, and restored.

My Father's Heart[1]

"I was born into a Catholic home," said Toni, "where, during my early childhood, I experienced wonderful love and security. That all came to an end when I reached age ten and my dad left our family for another woman without warning.

"I tried to cope by acting tough, but feelings of humiliation and rejection haunted me. I went through high school with a deep sense of shame, hiding from what I considered to be the ugly fact that I was from a broken home.

"Mom, though excommunicated from the church because of her divorce, clung tenaciously to her belief that God was an important part of our lives, and made sure that all of us attended religion classes. As for me, I wondered why God had allowed such a terrible thing to happen to us.

"That question and many others troubled me until I came to a major turning point in my life: I accepted Jesus Christ as my Lord and Savior. Yielding my life to Him, I was on the way to becoming a new person—a complete person.

"Soon after my conversion, I enrolled as a student at Bethany College of Missions. It was there that I met my husband, Paul.

"As our wedding date drew near, I felt the Holy Spirit dealing with me to forgive my dad. I knew that unless I forgave him, the resentful feelings I had held toward him would eventually be turned toward my own husband.

"So I wrote Dad a letter, reminding him of better and happier times. But I also told him how much it had hurt when he left us and how humiliated and rejected I had felt. Then I told him that I had forgiven him and hoped for an immediate response. It never came.

"After Paul and I were married, we headed for the Philippines. Along with us went our six-month-old daughter, Kelli. She was later joined by our son, Tyler, who was born there.

"During that time there was little communication from my family. One of the few letters that arrived brought the sad news that Mom's cancer had taken a turn for the worse. Another told us that she had received Christ as her Savior. Six months later we were told that she had died.

"After seven years, we returned to the States and joined the home staff of Bethany Fellowship to help train and support foreign missionaries.

"At Bethany we observed some strong family relationships. I loved this at first, but after a while noticed a strange thing happening inside of me. As I saw the closeness, even between Paul and our daughter, Kelli, I would begin to feel the immensity of what I had missed as an older child.

"When I thought of my father, I felt that our relationship had died. I felt no ties, no support, and no closeness. A friend suggested that I seek ministry. So I called Jack and he agreed to see me the very next day.

"As Paul and I drove to the counseling session, I began to have doubts. Was it really necessary? After all I had not been abused as some women had.

"But once I met Jack my fears were relieved. I felt at ease and told him about my feelings of rejection and shame. He listened attentively and then suggested that we pray together.

"Suddenly, fear gripped my heart as I excused myself from the room. I was not unwilling to forgive, but neither was I ready to expose the intensity of my feelings to anyone. Finally, after a considerable struggle, I went back into the room and agreed to pray.

"Then Jack took the place of my dad. After hearing all of my complaints, he confessed his guilt and humbly asked me to forgive him.

"I was totally unprepared for that, and his request for forgiveness brought tears to my eyes. For the first time in my life I could understand what had happened in my family.

"No longer would I make unrealistic demands or hold unfilled expectations. I was accepted as I was before God the Father. Now I could accept others, including Dad, as they were.

"As I saw the greatness of God's Father-love, all the chains that had bound me to the past were cut and I knew I was free. I no longer had to worry about whether or not I had a family. I was a little girl in the arms of my adopted Daddy—my Heavenly Father.

"I now felt I could have a long talk with my own dad. It would be hard, but I knew God would help me. The next day, we were to have a family reunion, and I would have my chance.

"When we arrived at Granddad's house, I saw Dad and my stepmom and greeted them as usual. As we visited with the family, I looked for an opportunity to get Dad alone. Finally I walked over and asked if the two of us could go for a walk.

"As we left the house together, I felt like I was walking with a stranger. But I knew I had to pour out my heart to him and I had to tell him what my Heavenly Father had done for me.

"So we walked along the sidewalk in the old neighborhood where Dad had grown up. As soon as I felt able, I asked, 'Do you remember the letter I wrote just a couple of months before Paul and I were married? That's what I want to talk about.

"'Dad, did you know that the neighbors ridiculed us? Did you know that there were times when we only had oatmeal to eat? Did you know that I wanted you there to share in my accomplishments?'

"By then Daddy was crying and, of course, I was, too. Finally I said, 'What I really need to know is: Do you love me?'

"At that point Daddy took me in his arms. With tears running down his face he said, 'I love you so much! I'm glad you've come and talked to me. I didn't know how badly you were hurting. I'm sorry I wasn't there for you.'

"I was amazed at what my father was saying, because the words he used were almost identical to the words Jack had used the day before.

"There we stood on the sidewalk, holding each other tightly, with tears of joy bathing our cheeks and hearts. The wall between us finally had come down.

"And it's still down. I have a new relationship with my Heavenly Father, and my earthly father as well."

"Daddy, Can I Sit on Your Lap?"

One day Sandra came for ministry. "Jack, I believe I have gotten some insights into my past and I would like to have you pray with me.

"I believe that much of my anger and rebellion has been directed toward my father. He was so legalistic and demanding that I never really felt close to him. When I was a little girl I wanted to please him, but I never did.

"Finally I rebelled and began sleeping around with any guy who would have me. I could never understand why I was doing these things, but now I realize that I was trying to hurt my father.

"Thank God, that is past history. Since then Jesus has come into my heart and saved me! Now I want to serve Him in full-time ministry."

"Sandra," I said, "I feel I am to take your father's place and ask your forgiveness. You need to get rid of all these negative feelings and judgments that you have against your dad."

As we prayed, Father released His forgiving love in the depths of her being and Sandra wept. Then she cried for joy at the revelation of the Father's love for her as His child.

Finally I said, "I don't want to embarrass you, but do you think you could be a little girl who needs to sit on her daddy's lap?"

"Yes," she said.

As Sandra sat on my lap, she broke and wept some more. "You know I've always wanted to sit on my daddy's lap."

"Sandra," I said, "I believe the next time you see your dad you are going to do just that!"

A few months passed. Then I returned to the YWAM base to teach another seminar on the Father Heart of God. The night I arrived, Sandra came to see me.

"Jack, I have to tell you what happened! After my outreach I went home. Then I received a phone call, inviting me to return to the YWAM base as a staff member.

"So my family went with me to the airport to see me off. As we were waiting for the flight to be called, suddenly I felt this overwhelming desire to sit on my father's lap. So I went over to him and said, 'Daddy, can I sit on your lap?'

"I snuggled. Then I hugged him again and again. 'Daddy,' I said, 'I really, really love you.'

"My father looked at me and said, 'You really mean that, don't you? You really do love me.'"

Sandra was telling me this story on Saturday evening. It had happened just a few weeks before that.

Sunday at 7:30 P.M. she said, "My family just called. Daddy has had a severe heart attack. They want me to come home."

Three hours later her family called again. Her father had died.

Shocked, Sandra came to tell me the news. "Jack," she said, "I am so grateful that God brought about that healing and reconciliation in the airport terminal before my father died.

"I was really looking forward to having a relationship with my dad, like none I had ever known before. It's hard for me to realize that he's dead and that can never be.

"But I am so glad that I know God as my Father. That's a relationship that will never end!"

*The incredible thing about this story
is that Jesus is really talking about His own Father
and He's picturing Him as a man who RUNS
to meet His son.*

Chapter Four

The Homecoming

But while he was still a long way off, his father saw him and was filled with compassion for him; he ran to his son, threw his arms around him and kissed him.

Luke 15:20b

*H*ow many of us, like Sandra and the younger son, have rebelled against our parents, fallen into sin, and had to suffer the consequences of our behavior?

How many of us, when we've realized the mess we've gotten ourselves into, have gone to our parents, repented of our rebellious attitude, and sought restoration?

In Ephesians, the Apostle Paul says:

Children, obey your parents in the Lord, for this is right. "Honor your father and mother"—which is the first command-ment with a promise—"that it may go well with you and that you may enjoy long life on the earth."

Ephesians 6:1-3

Things did not go well for Sandra or the younger son. Should that surprise us, given what God's Word promises?

This may not be a popular subject in our day and age, when young people often rebel, leave home, and get into trouble. But it's important for all of us to realize that the outcome of such behavior has been and always will be the same.

Cursed is the man who dishonors his father or his mother.
Deuteronomy 27:16a

God's Word says if we dishonor our parents we will not be blessed, we will not live long on this earth, and things will not go well with us.

But praise God, this is not the end of the story! When we repent, there is forgiveness, restoration, and healing. This is what we see here, as the prodigal leaves the pigpen and turns his steps toward home.

Many, many times this father has looked down that road, waiting for his younger son's return. Seeing a figure in the distance, he has said, "Perhaps this is him. Perhaps this is my son." Then as the figure has come closer, he has recognized the form and with disappointment in his voice, said, "No, it's just one of my hired men coming in from the field."

But finally the day arrives—the day of the joyous homecoming! There in the distance, his head hanging down, defeated and ashamed, is his younger son. The father recognizes him at once and he runs. Yes, he RUNS to meet him!

The incredible thing about this story is that Jesus is really talking about His own Father and He's picturing Him as a man who RUNS to meet His son. As far as I know, it's the only place in Scripture where we see God running.

Then the father throws his arms around the prodigal and kisses him again and again and again. Literally, he smothers his son with kisses, even as his son is dressed in his filthy, smelly pig clothes!

When we come to the Father, that's how we come—in our sin and in our shame! There's no other way.

That's the hard part, isn't it? Many of us want to turn over a new leaf, put a few more dollars in the offering plate, and promise ourselves and God that we'll never sin again; but it doesn't work that way.

All of us have become like one who is unclean, and all our righteous acts are like filthy rags; we all shrivel up like a leaf, and like the wind our sins sweep us away.

Isaiah 64:6

Nothing we do can ever remove the awful filth and smell of the pigpen from our sinful lives. Only the Father can clean us up.

Now a lesser parent would have waited for the prodigal to arrive. He would have stood at the door and kept his distance.

A lesser parent would have outlined the conditions for his son's return. "You know, kid, you've really blown it. Look at all the pain you've inflicted upon your mother and me. We've been worrying night and day. Now here is what you have to do, if you want us to take you in."

A lesser parent would have waited for an apology to make sure his son was sincere. Surely he at least owed his father that much!

But our Heavenly Father, the One who is depicted in this parable, is not like that lesser parent. He does not keep His distance. He does not wait for an apology. He does not outline conditions for His son's return. Instead, filled with compassion, He RUNS, arms open wide, to receive him.

This is unconditional love, a love that meets the need. It doesn't even have to have a response. It is a love that penetrates and reaches the very heart. It is a love that changes, a love that never fails.

I don't think this younger son even knows how to handle his father's response, do you? He's expecting the worst, and that's what he deserves. He has slept with prostitutes. He has wasted his inheritance. He has even gone to the fields to feed swine. Instead he receives a joyous homecoming!

The son said to him, "Father, I have sinned against heaven and against you. I am no longer worthy to be called your son."

Luke 15:21

When we come to the Father, we come as we are—in our guilt and in our shame. But we also come in repentance, without excuse. Remember the words from that old hymn of invitation, *"Just As I Am,"* by Charlotte Elliott?

Just as I am, without one plea
But that Thy blood was shed for me,
And that Thou bidd'st me come to Thee,
O Lamb of God, I come! I come![2]

That's how the younger son comes to his father—WITHOUT ONE PLEA. He doesn't lie or try to justify his behavior. He gets right to the point. *"Father, I have sinned"* (v. 21).

The younger son is repentant. It's not a worldly sorrow that says, "I'm sorry I got caught. Father, forgive me." It's a godly sorrow that says, "I've sinned. Father, change me."

When sin comes between us and the one we love, fellowship is broken. It was true of the younger son and his father. It is true of us and our Heavenly Father. Now healing and restoration are needed.

The younger son humbles himself, acknowledges his sin, and asks for forgiveness, but not because his father demands that of him. His father's love is unconditional. Conscience demands that of him. Guilt has taken him captive.

So it is with us. We confess our sins not because the Father needs to hear our confession. We confess our sins because we need to be forgiven.

Guilt keeps our eyes focused on our navel. Guilt makes us stumble over words.

Only forgiveness can mend broken relationships and allow us to face the one we've wronged. Only forgiveness can allow us to get off the treadmill of regret and turn our eyes toward God.

"*I have sinned against heaven and against you. I am no longer worthy to be called your son*" (v. 21). That's all the prodigal says. Then his father cuts him short, calls in the servants, and has them prepare his son for the celebration!

We may want to rattle off a long list of sins, but Father is more interested in the condition of our heart. Are we repentant? Do we love Him? Are we ready to come home?

What does the younger son do in his confession? He admits his sin. But more importantly, he focuses on the broken relationship: "*I am no longer worthy to be called your son*" (v. 21).

The father knows his younger son has sinned. In fact, he has forgiven him even before he runs to meet him on the road. But in the father's eyes, his son is worthy. He does not need to become as one of the hired men.

Isn't that incredible? That's a picture of our Heavenly Father.

If we confess our sins, he is faithful and just and will forgive us our sins and purify us from all unrighteousness.

1 John 1:9

When we confess our sins, Father is faithful—true to His Word. He forgives our sins; washes us in the precious blood of His Son, the Lord Jesus Christ; and cleanses us from ALL unrighteousness.

In our Father's eyes we are worthy, but not because of anything we have done. We are worthy because of our faith in Jesus Christ and His death on the cross!

God made him who had no sin to be sin for us, so that in him
we might become the righteousness of God.

2 Corinthians 5:21

The scribes and Pharisees, who are listening as Jesus relates this parable, are surprised by the father's reaction to his younger son's sin. Perhaps we are, too.

That's because we have been listening to the subtle and vicious lies that Satan has been placing in our minds, telling us that we serve an angry God who wants to punish us for our every sin.

While most of us can relate to Jesus, especially as we see Him blessing the children, healing the lepers, or showing mercy to the woman caught in adultery, few of us can relate to the Father, who is seemingly out to get us!

What does Scripture have to say about this theological misconception?

And he passed in front of Moses, proclaiming, "The LORD, the
LORD, the compassionate and gracious God, slow to anger,
abounding in love and faithfulness, maintaining love to thou-
sands, and forgiving wickedness, rebellion and sin."

Exodus 34:6-7a

But you, O Lord, are a compassionate and gracious God, slow
to anger, abounding in love and faithfulness.

Psalm 86:15

Moses and David see God as compassionate, gracious, slow to anger, and abounding in love and faithfulness. Even though both of them—Moses in slaying the Egyptian (Exodus 2:11-14) and David in plotting Uriah's death (2 Samuel 11:14-17)—had been found guilty of murder!

This is a serious dilemma. How can we cultivate a relationship with the Father when we believe He is angry with us? We can't. We avoid people like that. Right?

God sent His Son not just to forgive us our sins so that we could go to heaven. (Though that is certainly part of it.) God sent Jesus to die for us so that He, God the Father, could have a close and personal relationship with each one of us.

That's why He created us—to have fellowship with Him. He loves us!

But when we reject that love and insist on going our own way, without the redemption that Jesus provides, Father allows us the freedom to choose. Then, like the father in the parable, He stands at the door and waits, longing for our return.

How much does Father love us? Enough to believe that none of us would ever reject that love!

> *Then I saw a great white throne and him who was seated on it.*
> *Earth and sky fled from his presence, and there was no place*
> *for them. And I saw the dead, great and small, standing before*
> *the throne, and books were opened.*
>
> Revelation 20:11-12a

That is why in the vision John experienced on the island of Patmos, there was found *"no place for them"!*

From the very beginning Father expected that we would receive His Son as Lord and Savior and desire a personal relationship with Him as our Father. So He prepared only one place for us—heaven!

Only through our willful, continual refusal to respond to His love will we force Him to send us to *Gehenna*, the place He has prepared for Satan and his angels.

> *Therefore, O house of Israel, I will judge you, each one accord-*
> *ing to his ways, declares the Sovereign LORD. Repent! Turn*
> *away from all your offenses; then sin will not be your downfall.*
> *Rid yourselves of all the offenses you have committed, and get a*
> *new heart and a new spirit. Why will you die, O house of*
> *Israel? For I take no pleasure in the death of anyone, declares*
> *the Sovereign LORD. Repent and live!*
>
> Ezekiel 18:30-32

God does not want us to spend eternity in hell. He wants us to repent, receive a new heart and a new spirit, and live with Him forever!

Can we see our Heavenly Father, like the father in the parable, standing at the door, waiting, longing for our return? In love and compassion He will RUN to meet us, if we turn our steps toward home!

"Come into My Heart..." [3]

When I first met Tom, he was rebellious and very angry. Caring little how his behavior affected his family or those who were deeply concerned for him, he had become a law unto himself.

"I want to do my own thing," said Tom, "in my own way, in my own time."

It was a life of struggle, turmoil, and heartache. Tom was hanging out with the wrong crowd, getting into all kinds of trouble—at home, at school, and in his community.

The day he came to me for counsel, he was afraid. A girl he had been dating was saying that he was the father of her child.

"I know it isn't true," Tom said, "but I don't know what the result is going to be."

We talked about the situation. Then we prayed, and Father began a work in his rebellious heart.

Tom had been brought up in a Christian home, but all his godly parents had been able to do for him was pray. He was unwilling to listen or submit to any kind of authority.

A few weeks later Tom attended a young people's meeting. As the leader asked for some song requests, Tom raised his hand. He wanted to sing that little chorus by Harry D. Clarke, "Come into my heart, Lord Jesus." [4]

"As we sang," said Tom, "Father touched my heart and broke through my rebellious attitude. After the campfire I went back to my cabin. I knew that God was working in my life. I knew that He was calling me unto Himself.

"A few days later I asked the Lord to forgive me, come into my heart, and take complete control of my life. It was a powerful conversion. From that moment on I knew my life was different.

"My mom said later that someone had called her from camp and told her that I had given my heart to the Lord. After all the pain I had caused her, my conversion seemed too good to be true. She said she felt she needed to see me before she could believe that Father had answered her prayers."

When camp was over, Tom's dad came to pick him up. There in the parking lot I watched as, running to meet each other, they embraced and openly wept in each other's arms.

Tom's father and mother had spent many years interceding for their son in prayer—longing, hoping, waiting for his return. Finally, Father in His love and mercy had reached down and touched Tom's life. Their son had come home.

Since then Tom has been serving the Lord full time, both on the mission field and as a staff member at Bethany College of Missions.

"Lord, If You're Real—
Prove It!"

"Our Heavenly Father says, '*When you search for Me with all your heart... I will be found by you*' (Jeremiah 29:13b-14a, AMP). How true this is! After many years of seeking with my whole heart, God found me and I found Him," said Joe.

"My search for an intimate relationship with the Lord began at a very early age in the Catholic Church. I longed to know the Lord and to serve Him, but no one in my denomination nurtured that desire or gave me instruction. All I knew was to follow the religious tradition of my parents.

"Wanting to serve God and His people, I thought the priesthood would be the best way to do that. So from an early age I pursued that calling in all of my endeavors.

"After eight years of preparation in college and seminary, I was ordained to the Roman Catholic priesthood. I carried a tremendous inferiority complex into my pastoral work, and was literally frightened to preach and to perform many of my priestly duties. In fact, my last year of seminary I almost chose to go with the brothers to avoid having to face my fears.

"Finally, after seven years of service, my frustration became unbearable. I had done all of the right things: I had been baptized as an infant, confirmed as a teenager, and graduated from our church college and seminary. Yet my heart was empty.

"I cried out to the Lord, 'If You're real, prove it!!! I know all about You, but something is missing.'

"I did not have the intimate relationship that comes from receiving Christ into my heart and making Him Lord of all. I felt like a hired servant. I was being used by the church, but did not know that I was loved or that I could have a personal relationship with God.

"Not long after I prayed that prayer, I was assigned to a country church as a pastor. Not having the duties of a parochial school, I was able to seek the Lord in a more intense way. I continued my search for Him in my meditation, private and public prayers, study of theology, and in the Word.

"Shortly after I moved, an Assembly of God pastor began to share the Gospel with me. 'I know you love God and His people,' the pastor said. 'Why don't you just ask God to come into your life? Give your whole self to Him.'

"Though I resisted for several months, the Holy Spirit began to bring conviction. I would lie awake at night pondering many things. The Scriptures began to burn in my heart as I was confronted with the need to surrender my life completely to Christ.

"I prayed a prayer over and over for nine months, asking Jesus to come into my life. I did not know that the first time I prayed it sincerely I was truly 'born again,' but I did begin to change. Had God not met me, I probably would have left the priesthood.

"For two years following this experience I had such a hunger for the Word that I studied the New Testament with great intensity. The Holy Spirit made God's Word alive to me and brought much understanding and truth to my heart. I needed His reassurance because I knew no one in my church denomination who had had this type of conversion experience.

"My newfound faith changed my life. I wasn't put out of the priesthood. In fact, my bishop commended me for doing such a 'good job of teaching' in the high school.

"The Word of God came alive as I shared it from the pulpit. Some people, who didn't like what the Lord was doing in and through me, turned away and left the parish. Others liked the change and began to seek a personal relationship with the Lord for themselves.

"As I brought everything to the Lord and allowed the Holy Spirit to lead me, He began to release me from my fear of rejection. Now I am growing in confidence as I experience what He is able to do in and through me.

"As a result, my ministry is more relaxed, productive, and exciting. For so many years I had lived with the fear of being a failure.

"Now as God's child I know His love for me is not dependent upon performance. It is unconditional because of what Christ has done for me at Calvary.

" I have a compassion and a Christlike love for others. The Lord has brought so much understanding and wholeness to me that now I am able to effectively help others. I see them find Christ, become filled with the Holy Spirit, and begin a journey toward spiritual maturity.

"When I entered the priesthood, I felt I was serving God. But now I realize that all I was doing was serving a religious system. As a Roman Catholic, it was all I knew.

"Now I have a holy passion to win souls for Christ and to minister to God's people on all levels, clergy and laypeople alike. I want to see the body of Christ come together in the unity of the Holy Spirit and the revelation of the Father's love so that we will be prepared for Christ's soon return for us as His bride."

No price, including the death of His Son on the cross, is too high for the Father to pay. He will do whatever He has to do to reclaim that which has been lost.

Chapter Five

Lost and Found

"For this son of mine was dead and is alive again; he was lost and is found." So they began to celebrate.

Luke 15:24

The scribes and the Pharisees are perplexed, angered. Why can't Jesus get to the point? Why can't He give them a straight answer once and for all?

This is the third time that He has gone off on a tangent, telling them a story about something that is "lost." First it was a sheep. Then it was a coin. Now it is a son.

God have mercy should there be a fourth parable! A lost goat? A lost daughter? A lost plow?

The accusation is a simple one. It's a large crowd. Suddenly these tax collectors and "sinners" come and join in with the throng.

But the Pharisees and the teachers of the law muttered, "This man welcomes sinners and eats with them."

Luke 15:2

What's wrong with this Jesus of Nazareth? Why is He spending His time talking and eating with the absolute scum of the earth? Now that is something that no religious leader would do, let alone the Son of God!

What the scribes and the Pharisees don't know, let alone understand, is that Jesus is responding to their accusation. He has heard them and is grieved.

Later, in chapter 19, when Jesus dines with the tax collector, Zacchaeus, He will face a similar accusation:

> *All the people saw this and began to mutter, "He has gone to be*
> *the guest of a 'sinner.'"*
>
> Luke 19:7

His response, as Zacchaeus offers to give half of his possessions to the poor and to pay back four times what is owed to anyone he has cheated, will be the same. Jesus will make yet another reference to "the lost."

> *Jesus said to him [Zacchaeus], "Today salvation has come to*
> *this house, because this man, too, is a son of Abraham. For the*
> *Son of Man came to seek and to save what was lost."*
>
> Luke 19:9-10

For this is Jesus' mission, His goal in life—to seek and to save that which is lost!

What the scribes and the Pharisees also fail to understand is that Jesus is speaking not only to them, but about them. It's not just the tax collectors and the "sinners" that are lost. They, the religious leaders of the day, also are in need of a Savior.

How can this be? Let's go back to the beginning, where Jesus relates the parable of the lost sheep.

> *Then Jesus told them this parable: "Suppose one of you has a*
> *hundred sheep and loses one of them. Does he not leave the*
> *ninety-nine in the open country and go after the lost sheep until*
> *he finds it? And when he finds it, he joyfully puts it on his*
> *shoulders and goes home. Then he calls his friends and neigh-*
> *bors together and says, 'Rejoice with me; I have found my lost*
> *sheep.' I tell you that in the same way there will be more rejoic-*
> *ing in heaven over one sinner who repents than over ninety-*
> *nine righteous persons who do not need to repent."*
>
> Luke 15:3-7

A sheep is an animal that is stupid, helpless, easily frightened, and totally dependent upon its shepherd. It has no sense of direction and when it wanders off, it is lost until the shepherd comes and finds it—usually in a waterless hollow or a mountain ravine—and bears it home, carrying it on his shoulders.

The Bible says we all, like sheep, have gone astray:

We all, like sheep, have gone astray, each of us has turned to
his own way; and the LORD has laid on him [Jesus] the iniquity
of us all.

Isaiah 53:6

No longer in the care of Jesus, the Good Shepherd, we have allowed
another—Satan, the father of lies—to come over the wall of the sheepfold
and lure us away. Jesus said:

I tell you the truth, the man who does not enter the sheep pen
by the gate, but climbs in by some other way, is a thief and a
robber.

John 10:1

I [Jesus] am the gate; whoever enters through me will be
saved. He will come in and go out, and find pasture. The
thief [Satan] comes only to steal and kill and destroy; I have
come that they may have life, and have it to the full. I am the
good shepherd. The good shepherd lays down his life for the
sheep.

John 10:9-11

Then, like helpless lambs, our eyes blinded and our hearts deadened to the
truth of God, we are led to the slaughter.

For this reason they could not believe, because, as Isaiah says
elsewhere: "He [Satan] has blinded their eyes and deadened
their hearts, so they can neither see with their eyes, nor under-
stand with their hearts, nor turn—and I would heal them."

John 12:39-40

A sheep that leaves the fold and wanders off on its own is easy prey,
not only for a wild animal but also for a thief and a robber. This is what
happens when the prodigal leaves the structure and safety of his father's
house and his Jewish community. Blinded to the truth, he becomes easy
prey for all that Satan has to offer and, like a helpless lamb, he is slowly
led to the slaughter.

How many sheep does this shepherd have? How many wander off and
are lost?

Would we leave a flock of sheep in open country and take whatever risks are necessary to find just one lone straggler? Perhaps not.

Taking an objective, bottom-line approach to this business venture, we might decide to stay with the flock. After all, we still have 99 sheep. What is the loss of one compared to the safety of the others?

This is an economy that defies objective reasoning. It's a radical view of life called the Kingdom of God where even one sheep is sought by its Heavenly Father until it is found.

Why? It is valued. It is precious in the sight of God.

Though the sheep wanders off through sheer stupidity, the prodigal who is headstrong and rebellious makes a deliberate decision to leave. Both endure a life of misery and hardship while they are lost. Both are the reason for rejoicing when they are found!

The second story that Jesus shares with the crowd is the parable of the lost coin.

> *Or suppose a woman has ten silver coins and loses one. Does she not light a lamp, sweep the house and search carefully until she finds it? And when she finds it, she calls her friends and neighbors together and says, "Rejoice with me; I have found my lost coin." In the same way, I tell you, there is rejoicing in the presence of the angels of God over one sinner who repents.*
> Luke 15:8-10

In Bible times, when a bride's parents would give their daughter in marriage, the marriage would be seen as decreasing the efficiency of the bride's family and increasing the efficiency of the groom's family, as often unmarried women would tend the flock (Exodus 2:16), work in the fields, or help in some other way.

To adequately compensate the family for this loss, the groom would be expected to provide a "dowry." This could be paid in cash. Or, as it was in the case of Jacob, it could be paid in service.

> *Jacob was in love with Rachel and said, "I'll work for you seven years in return for your younger daughter Rachel."*
> Genesis 29:18

This is not to say that women were merely property to be purchased. The bride also received a portion of this dowry, in addition to any personal gifts or special marriage dowry—such as the damsels and nurse that were given to Rebekah (Genesis 24:59,61), and the field of springs of water that Caleb gave his daughter (Judges 1:15)—that the parents might provide.

The bride was seen as a property owner, an independent person who was coming into the relationship as a valued partner with her husband. Any gifts or personal dowry she might bring into the marriage would remain hers should the marriage fail and there be a divorce.

In New Testament times, it also was common for a father to give his daughter a gift of coins, with holes drilled in them so they could be worn on a string.

This is no doubt why this woman in Jesus' parable is so distraught. The coin she has lost is part of her wealth, or marriage dowry, most likely worn on the front of her high cap which, with her veil, would form her headdress.

It would have to be a dire circumstance for her to part with such a coin. Not to mention the evil meaning that would be attached to such a loss, should it occur, and the resulting shame.

What does this woman do when she discovers that the coin has been lost? She lights a lamp, sweeps the house, and searches carefully until she finds it. Then she calls her friends and neighbors together and says, *"Rejoice with me"* (v. 9).

Why? The coin is valued. It is part of her inheritance.

In just such a way the lost sheep, the lost coin, and the lost son are the wealth of the Father. Out of His perfect love He has created them, and they are His inheritance—valued, precious in His sight.

No price, including the death of His Son on the cross, is too high for the Father to pay. He will do whatever He has to do to reclaim that which has been lost. Then when it is found, He will throw a party as all the angels of heaven look on and rejoice!

For the righteous? No, for the sinner!

Why are the Pharisees lost? They do not value what God has created, what is closest to His heart: all mankind. They are no better, nor are they any worse in the eyes of God than the men they openly despise: the tax collectors and the sinners. That is the ultimate deception.

The Pharisees are sheep without a shepherd, an inheritance that has been lost in the darkness, and elder sons who refuse to join in the party.

But God loves them anyway. He just wants them to come home.

"Now My Family Comes First!"

When Insook came that day for prayer, I could tell by the sad look in her eyes that she was deeply troubled.

"Jack," she said, "I have something I need to confess.

"Twelve years ago when Limsoo asked me to marry him, like any bride-to-be, I was beaming from ear to ear. My joy was so great I could hardly wait to get home and share the wonderful news with my family, my friends—with anyone who would stop, listen, and admire my beautiful diamond ring!

"Yet, at the same time, I was afraid. I had a secret, a sin from my past that I had been too ashamed to share, either with my family or with Limsoo. Only my best girlfriend, Soo Hee, knew what I had done, and I was concerned that even she might betray me with a smile, an unconscious word, or even a gesture before the day of the ceremony.

"You see, I was not a virgin. In my country that is a sin which is not taken lightly by any man.

"Limsoo loved me, but he was also an honorable man. I knew that if he were ever to find out what I had done, he would feel dishonored and would call off our engagement.

"So I did not tell him, and that lie has kept me from being a happy wife.

"When you said that the secret of intimacy with the Father and with one another is 'walking in the light,' God showed me what I must to do. If I want to experience the emotional honesty and closeness you say is possible with my husband, Limsoo, I must tell him the truth.

"But he is a very angry man. I know that he will never forgive me."

I prayed with Insook, but she was still too afraid to tell her husband the truth. So a couple of months passed before I saw her again. Then she came, determined that she had to face him, no matter what the cost. So I agreed to be in the room with her when she finally told him what had happened.

Insook was right. Limsoo was not only angry, he was furious. "I never thought I was married to *that* kind of woman," he said, as he turned his back and stormed out of the room, slamming the door behind him.

A man of very few words, Limsoo did not know what to say or what to do in light of such a confession. He was shocked, to put it mildly. How could Insook have dishonored him and his family? Should he divorce her for lying to him? No, he loved her too much to do that.

For weeks Limsoo struggled. Late at night he would grab his pillow and blanket from their bedroom, retreat to the den, and begin to pace the floor.

Just a few months before he, too, had become a Christian. Now God was asking him to forgive his wife in the same way that he himself had been forgiven. Was that a reasonable request? Was that something he could even do?

A few months later when I saw Limsoo, he said: "Jack, I just could not understand. After Insook told me everything, she was so happy and I was so miserable.

"In the past, I had done everything I could think of to make her happy. I had bought her a new house, with a small wooded area in the back for flowers and a vegetable garden. I had bought her a new car with bucket seats, air conditioning, and a wall-to-wall stereo system. But nothing I said or did seemed to help.

"There was always a sadness about her. She would look at me, but I knew without asking that her mind and heart were miles away—in another time, another place.

"Many nights I would think of saying to Insook, 'What's wrong? Tell me why you are so troubled.' But having been brought up to believe that an honorable man provides for his family, tenderness and gentle words have never been easy for me. I like to buy things and do things for Insook. But inside I know she just wants me to spend time with her and talk.

"Then one day she calls me into this room, confesses that she has lied to me, and she is happy! Women—who can understand them?

"But I am glad that the deception has been exposed. It is wonderful to be married to a happy wife! Now Insook is free from the shame of her past.

"I wish I could say it was easy for me to forgive, but as a new Christian, Father really had to deal with my heart. Now I realize that it took great courage for Insook to call me into that room, and that by telling me the truth she was truly honoring me, both as her husband and as the father of her children.

"All of this has brought great change to our family. Before, I was not a considerate husband, nor was I a loving father to my children. Work was the most important thing in my life. Now my family comes first!

"When people see the change, they say, 'Limsoo, you are a happy man. You have a happy wife. What is the secret?'

"I smile and say, 'We always "walk in the light." ' Then I tell them what God has done.

"There are so many families that need this kind of help. Now that Father has brought forgiveness and healing to my house, I want to share what He has done with others. I want every man I know to have a happy wife!"

"Father's Tears Washed Me!"

"It was during group prayer time," said Robin, "when we were releasing family members from any hurts that they had caused us, that God spoke to me. I remembered the many times that my dad had hit Mummy and me.

"Nothing was pleasant. I didn't want to remember. Hurting deep inside, I was finding it very hard to forgive my dad, and was fighting with Daddy God.

"'I can't forgive him,' I said. 'I don't want to forgive him. I'll never forgive him.'

"I was wrestling with my emotions as I tried to bottle up the tears that were flooding out. God's love never ceased to reach out to my soft, hurting heart.

"The little boy in me came alive, and I forgave Dad through clenched teeth.

"It was then that my heart broke and I wept and wept.

"Father God met this little boy—yes, me! It was then that I was aware that my hands were raised and I was reaching to the Father. I sensed God's tears running down my hands and all over my body. Daddy God was crying!

"'Why are you crying, Daddy God?' I asked.

"He replied, 'I saw your little body hurting, and I've been hurting all this time. Today I want to wash you clean and remove all the pain.'

"God's tears were warm and salty, just like mine. I felt clean and free. I knew it was true.

"God spoke again. This time I had a sense that I was kneeling before my own father. My head was cupped in his hands and, as I wept, my tears were running down his big hands. I was only a little boy.

"I was washing my dad's hands clean—no longer were they dirty from hitting me and hurting me. I had forgiven him for what he had done to Mum and me.

"Just as Father God's tears washed me clean, by my tears I had washed my dad's hands clean. I had once and for all forgiven him.

"Hallelujah! Praise God! I am loved and fathered by the true and living God!"

What is grace? It is God running to meet our need. It is His ability in us. When we come to the end of our resources, as the prodigal came to the end of his, we can go to the throne of God and receive what we need from the Father.

Chapter Six

Restored by Grace

But the father said to his servants, "Quick! Bring the best robe and put it on him. Put a ring on his finger and sandals on his feet. Bring the fattened calf and kill it. Let's have a feast and celebrate. For this son of mine was dead and is alive again; he was lost and is found." So they began to celebrate.

Luke 15:22-24

What follows the younger son's confession? A public form of humiliation? A full-blown lecture? A cool stare? No, a party complete with barbecued beef!

It's always a surprise, as it was for Insook, Robin's father, and the prodigal, when punishment is withheld. But that is the mystery and the wonder of God's amazing grace!

Mosaic Law demands that a son who curses his father or mother be put to death:

Anyone who curses his father or mother must be put to death.

Exodus 21:17

and that a stubborn and rebellious son be stoned:

They shall say to the elders, "This son of ours is stubborn and rebellious. He will not obey us. He is a profligate and a drunkard." Then all the men of his town shall stone him to death.

Deuteronomy 21:20-21a

So why, in the midst of all this sin, would the father throw a party?

For the scribes and the Pharisees, this outcome is not only an outrage, but also a source for heated debate. Instead of the tragic ending (death) the Law requires, this younger son receives what he does not deserve: a new beginning (life)!

But in this parable of the prodigal son, Jesus is not only revealing the love of the Father, He is also heralding the arrival of the New Covenant, foretold over 600 years before by the prophet Jeremiah.

"The time is coming," declares the LORD, *"when I will make a new covenant with the house of Israel and with the house of Judah…. "I will put my law in their minds and write it on their hearts. I will be their God, and they will be my people. No longer will a man teach his neighbor, or a man his brother, saying, 'Know the* LORD,' *because they will all know me, from the least of them to the greatest," declares the* LORD. *"For I will forgive their wickedness and will remember their sins no more."*

Jeremiah 31:31,33b-34

The New Covenant will finally do what the Jewish people have never been able to do on their own. It will fulfill the demands of the Law by providing the perfect sacrifice, once for all.

First he [Jesus] said, "Sacrifices and offerings, burnt offerings and sin offerings you did not desire, nor were you pleased with them" (although the law required them to be made). Then he [Jesus] said, "Here I am, I have come to do your will." He sets aside the first to establish the second. And by that will, we have been made holy through the sacrifice of the body of Jesus Christ once for all.

Hebrews 10:8-10

Fortunately for all of us, the Old Covenant (Mosaic Law) was not God's last word to man. It was only a temporary measure until a New Covenant (grace) with a better sacrifice (Jesus Christ) could be provided.

That is not to say that as Christians we are exempt from living a righteous life before God, using the moral guidelines provided in the Ten Commandments. Jesus said:

> *Do not think that I have come to abolish the Law or the*
> *Prophets; I have not come to abolish them but to fulfill them. I*
> *tell you the truth, until heaven and earth disappear, not the*
> *smallest letter, not the least stroke of a pen, will by any means*
> *disappear from the Law until everything is accomplished.*
>
> Matthew 5:17-18

What it does mean is that when we sin, we have a "new" way to come to the Father—through the blood of His Son, the Lord Jesus Christ.

That is why this younger son can be forgiven and set free from the penalty of death! When the Kingdom of God is ushered in through Jesus' death on the cross, a New Covenant will be established that will allow the demands of the Law to be met through a perfect sacrifice: the Lamb of God.

What a glorious truth! If only the religious leaders could comprehend what Jesus is saying. But for them grace is a new concept, an idea that is foreign to their legalistic stance.

Yes, they have seen grace demonstrated from time to time in the Old Testament when God has withheld judgment, but it has been the exception, not the rule, under Mosaic Law.

The Law, says Paul, reveals our sinful nature and makes us conscious of sin.

> *Now we know that whatever the law says, it says to those who*
> *are under the law, so that every mouth may be silenced and the*
> *whole world held accountable to God. Therefore no one will be*
> *declared righteous in his sight by observing the law; rather,*
> *through the law we become conscious of sin.*
>
> Romans 3:19-20

But it can never make us righteous before a Holy God, nor was it ever intended to do so.

> *But now a righteousness from God, apart from law, has been*
> *made known, to which the Law and the Prophets testify. This*
> *righteousness from God comes through faith in Jesus Christ to*
> *all who believe. There is no difference, for all have sinned and*
> *fall short of the glory of God.*
>
> Romans 3:21-23

Faith has always been God's way of salvation. Abraham, who lived some 400 years before the Law was even introduced, had a personal relationship with God because he believed God *"and it was credited to him as righteousness"* (Romans 4:3b).

What is grace? It is God running to meet our need. It is His ability in us. When we come to the end of our resources, as the prodigal came to the end of his, we can go to the throne of God and receive what we need from the Father.

> *Let us then fearlessly* and *confidently* and *boldly draw near to the throne of grace (the throne of God's unmerited favor to us sinners), that we may receive mercy [for our failures] and find grace to help in good time for every need [appropriate help and well-timed help, coming just when we need it].*
>
> Hebrews 4:16, AMP

It is the blood of Christ that gives us boldness. Then all we have to do is humble ourselves and ask.

That's what the younger son does. He humbles himself, comes to his father, and asks for what he needs: forgiveness and restoration. Then his father does the rest.

Let's suppose that we pull into a gas station and say, "Fill 'er up!" Then we leave before the attendant has had a chance to put the needed gas in our tank.

What's going to happen? A few miles down the road, we're going to find ourselves out of gas, thumbing a ride to the nearest station! Right?

Are we responding to the Father in the same way that we responded to that attendant? Are we coming to Him for grace, then leaving before He can fill us up?

The throne of God is like a 24-hour full-service gas station. When we pull in, we can get gas (grace), oil (the Spirit), a wash (cleansing), a map (direction), food (the Word), a new pump (heart), a brake job (restraint), a tune-up (forgiveness), or a complete overhaul (unconditional love).

Father is the Chief Mechanic. Even if we don't know what is wrong or what needs to be fixed, He does. We come to Him. We ask for His help. Then He does whatever needs to be done so we can head back onto the open road.

The cost? Well, we can forget our checkbooks, credit cards, and cash.

Only the precious blood of the Lord Jesus Christ will allow the Father to stamp our invoice "Paid in Full!" Everything in that station—parts, lubricants, accessories, even service—is our inheritance as sons and daughters of the Heavenly Father.

Are we coming to the throne of God in time of need? Are we asking the Father to fill us up?

Full-service, the grace station is open 24 hours a day, seven days a week, but we have to humble ourselves and ask. There's no pump marked "Self-serve"!

If we wait until our tank is on "empty" or until our car is stalled on the side of the road, Father is gracious. He will send someone—a close friend, a pastor, a husband or wife, sometimes even an angel—to tow us in. But it may be costly in terms of time lost on the road, while our life remains dismantled, hoisted on the rack for all who pass by to see.

Preventative maintenance is always best. It's when we hesitate or try to fix things on our own, that we fail to understand the meaning of grace.

At this station, Father does it all! It is His ability in and through us that keeps us going!

The Law demands; grace gives. The Law requires; grace promises. The Law condemns; grace sets free.

What the younger son cannot do for himself, through love and grace his father does for him. He gives his son a clean slate, a new beginning. He cancels the debt (sin) and the penalty (death) that is against him. Then he celebrates his return with a feast, complete with barbecued beef!

Yes, the father is as much a prodigal as is his younger son. The son is recklessly extravagant in his spending, but here we see that the father is just as lavish and just as extravagant in his love for his son.

The father gives him his best robe (the robe of honor worn on festive occasions), a ring for his finger (perhaps a signet, denoting family authority), and sandals (usually worn by sons and not by servants) for his feet.

Then the father has his servants prepare the very best foods, even a fattened calf, so the family can celebrate the younger son's return. A surprise, to be sure, for this fun-loving son who could never have imagined that his own father would throw the best party a son could ever have!

Remarkable, isn't it? The father doesn't even tell the servants to give the prodigal a bath before he receives him! He accepts him as he is. Why? In the father's eyes his son is forgiven. He has already been cleansed.

That's how our Heavenly Father sees us when we come to Him in repentance, washed in the blood of the Lamb!

> *In him we have redemption through his blood, the forgiveness*
> *of sins, in accordance with the riches of God's grace that he*
> *lavished on us with all wisdom and understanding.*
>
> Ephesians 1:7-8

This, too, must be hard for the younger son to receive. He comes home, expecting the worst and fearing his father's rejection. Instead he is forgiven and fully restored. It is a joyous homecoming!

Not only does it take humility for us to ask for forgiveness, but it also takes humility for us to receive that forgiveness when it's extended to us. That's not easy. A part of us wants to be punished. A part of us wants to pay for what we've done.

That's the difference between Mosaic Law and New Testament grace. Under Law we offer the sacrifice for sin. Under grace we accept the sacrifice that God has provided: the Lamb of God.

> *When you were dead in your sins...God made you alive with*
> *Christ. He forgave us all our sins, having canceled the written*
> *code, with its regulations, that was against us and that stood*
> *opposed to us; he took it away, nailing it to the cross.*
>
> Colossians 2:13-14

Jesus cancels the judgment (the Law) that is against us by taking our debt (sin) upon Himself and paying the penalty (death) in our place by His death on the cross.

That's what happens here. The father cancels the judgment, and grace sets the prodigal free!

Part III:
The Older Son

"I Owe It to Others"

"When I graduated from high school, I joined a missionary organiza-tion," said Sue. "For ten years I had many wonderful experiences in many different nations. Then I experienced burnout.

"No longer efficient in what I was doing, I did not have the physical or the emotional energy I needed to take care of myself and to serve oth-ers at the same time. But I pushed myself to perform.

"I began to search my heart. 'Lord, where is our relationship? I am so caught up in busyness that I no longer have time for You.

"'I have sacrificed. I have been faithful. I have given myself to oth-ers. But am I loved just for who I am?'

"A few years before, the Lord had given me a vision of a computer data base that would provide needed information on people groups around the world. When I shared my vision with those in authority, I was encour-aged to 'go for it!'

"Then, as time passed, I found that no one was providing the time or the resources I needed. More immediate projects were taking its place. It seemed like a mixed message: 'Go for your vision, but fulfill my vision first.'

"Because of my training and my background, I had always looked to leadership for direction and encouragement. I had been taught 'to lay down my life'—to pour out everything to take care of the needs of others and expect nothing in return.

"Suddenly I found myself asking, 'Does anyone care about me? Did I really hear from God? Is this vision to facilitate and disseminate a data base of information for missionaries just my own idea? God, why aren't You providing me with the time and the resources that are needed?'

"I became more and more frustrated. I was so project-oriented, that my value as a person was tied to performance. When I wasn't working hard and achieving results, I was uneasy. I felt I was letting myself, God, and others down.

"I took a one-year sabbatical from my responsibilities to take care of my ailing grandparents. It was a difficult time for me emotionally, but also a time of great blessing. I was able to serve my grandparents out of unconditional love, expecting nothing in return because of their love for me.

"God began to show me my heart. I had been striving, working hard because I felt I owed it to others—those who were supporting me and those who were over me. I wasn't serving the Lord out of a heart of love. I was serving others out of a sense of obligation.

"Even in my relationship with God I had been caught in a performance trap. I had felt that His love for me was in direct proportion to the number of hours I spent each day in Bible reading, prayer, soul-winning, and other ministry-related activities.

"Then I experienced grace! Father showed me that His love is not dependent on anything I do or don't do. His love is unconditional. It's a free gift that brings fulfillment.

"Father loves me just because I am His daughter. I can stop striving, stop performing, and just rest, trusting in Him completely.

"I have also come to realize that when God gives a vision, He also gives an anointing to fulfill a vision. For too many years I had been trying to do in my own strength what He wanted to accomplish through me in His strength.

"Now I feel I have the call of Nehemiah on my life, to minister to ministers—to restore and bring new life to burnt stones. So many of God's people are pouring out without knowing how to receive.

"Father is inviting the older sons into the party for a refreshing, a refocusing of vision, and a restoration of relationship. I, too, have joined in the celebration as He has been serving the new wine of His kingdom to thirsty souls throughout the world.

> *And afterward, I will pour out my Spirit on all people. Your*
> *sons and daughters will prophesy, your old men will dream*
> *dreams, your young men will see visions.*
>
> Joel 2:28

"As I yield to His Spirit and stop trying to figure everything out, I am finding tremendous love, joy, and peace in the Father's presence as I come to know Him for who He is. It's a heart relationship that is setting me free!"

"I Tried to Kill My Father"

"When I was three years old," said Yoon Chan, "I had a case of polio which affected both of my legs. As a result of the doctor's medicine and my mother's daily massage, eventually I was able to use my left leg. My mother also wanted me to have surgery on my right leg, but my father refused.

"I was seven when my mother was having tea with a close friend and I overheard her say, 'My husband refused to let him have the surgery. "We have three sons," he said. "We don't need this one."'

"Suddenly I felt this anger rise up in me. At first I wanted to die. Then I wanted to kill him.

"The anger and pain of rejection was so strong that I got into many fights as a child. The other children in my neighborhood would laugh and imitate my crippled walk. When I wanted to play with them, they would refuse to include me in their games.

"In Korea there is very little understanding or compassion for a handicapped child. So I felt I had to be tough to overcome my disadvantage.

"I always dreaded the days when as a family we would go to the bathhouse. I was ashamed of my body. I did not want others, even my own family, to look upon my naked body and make fun of me or add to my shame.

"My anger, my need to seek revenge kept me alive. I hated my father and his refusal to give me the medical care that I needed. No matter what I did or what I said to win his love and approval, he never accepted me. He only saw my deformed leg, my handicap.

"My anger grew until one night I decided to follow through on my plan. In a drunken rage I tried to kill my father and failed.

"A few years later, while I was a student at the university, I became a Christian. I began to serve the Lord in campus ministry, but had many emotional struggles.

"Then I married and had a son of my own. But before I knew it, the anger I'd had for my father began to come out toward my son. I was afraid.

"Jack, when you spoke from Psalm 139 about the Father's love:

For you created my inmost being; you knit me together in my mother's womb. I praise you because I am fearfully and wonderfully made.

Psalm 139:13-14a

the words struck my heart like a sledgehammer. I cried and cried and cried.

"Later when we prayed, Father gave me a heart of compassion for my father. His own mother had died when he was three years old, and his father had died four years later when he was seven. My father did not know how to love me as a son. He had never received the love he had needed as a child.

"Now my father and I have a real relationship, one that is based on love and mercy.

"Secure in the knowledge that God is my Father, I no longer have a need to take my childhood anger out on my son. He has given me a tender heart towards my son, one that is full of understanding, love, and compassion.

"On my wedding night I was so afraid that my body would be repulsive to my bride. Now I accept my body and my wife accepts me. I am able to go to the bathhouse or beach without shame.

"I am blessed! I know that God is fair and God is love. Father accepts me just the way I am. I no longer have to be strong. I am strong in the Lord!"

What do we have to do to be loved?
NOTHING. Father does it all! We come.
We ask. We receive. Love is a gift,
not a reward for service.

Chapter Seven

A Servant or a Son?

*Meanwhile, the older son was in the field. When he came near
the house, he heard music and dancing. So he called one of the
servants and asked him what was going on. "Your brother has
come," he replied, "and your father has killed the fattened calf
because he has him back safe and sound." The older brother
became angry and refused to go in. So his father went out and
pleaded with him.*

Luke 15:25-28

When Lisa came to see me, she was angry, bitter, and emotionally rigid. On the staff of a large missionary organization, she had been serving the Lord for many years, but still did not know that she was good enough to be loved.

Lisa was caught in a performance cycle, trying harder and harder to please her Heavenly Father.

"What more do I have to do?" she kept asking Him. "Work 10, 12 hours a day before I can know that I am good enough to be loved? What more do I have to do?"

Lisa was serving faithfully in her Father's house, without really knowing His heart. How many of us, like Lisa and Sue, are trying to earn the Father's love and acceptance by "being good" and working hard?

Such is the case with this older son. He is the "good boy" who stays on his father's farm and does whatever his father tells him to do. But when his brother, the "black sheep" of the family, comes home, his mask is suddenly torn off and he is seen for what he really is—a young man who has been "good" for all the wrong reasons.

Love flows out of relationship. When we know that we are loved and accepted just for who we are, apart from anything we do, then obedience becomes a heart response—a joyful willingness to do God's will.

> *Love the LORD your God with all your heart and with all your soul and with all your strength. These commandments that I give you today are to be upon your hearts.*
>
> Deuteronomy 6:5-6

But when our obedience is based on fear or a desire for personal reward, our efforts miss the mark and breed resentment. Jesus said:

> *As the Father has loved me, so have I loved you. Now remain in my love. If you obey my commands, you will remain in my love, just as I have obeyed my Father's commands and remain in his love.*
>
> John 15:9-10

The older son's obedience is not a heart response to love. Compulsive and calculating, it flows out of fear and a desire for personal gain. So when his younger brother, who has wasted his inheritance and fallen captive to sin, is welcomed home and receives all that he, as the older son, has longed for and more, his resentment turns to anger and he refuses to join the party.

Grace can be offensive to the mind, but it also will reveal the heart.

If we have never fallen or known the shame and heartache of having to live with a past, we may openly despise God's goodness and limitless love for the repentant sinner. But Jesus came to seek and to save that which was LOST, and this includes both the backslidden Christian and the rebellious sinner.

Could we have run to meet the prodigal on the road? Could we have thrown our arms around him, kissed him again and again even as he was standing there in his filthy, smelly pig clothes? Could we have loved him unconditionally?

Or, like the older son, would we have been offended and refused to join the party?

As soon as the father hears that his older son has come in from the field, he goes out to meet him. Then he pleads with him to come and join in the celebration.

The father goes to his son. The older son does not come to his father. Oftentimes that's how it is. In love we humble ourselves, even to the point of accepting an accusation that is unjust or unwarranted, to heal a broken relationship.

But the older son is angry. In fact, his anger, having festered over time, has become a root of bitterness. After all, this young man, this brother of his, is breaking his father's heart.

Yes, the older son knows all about it. Stories of immorality, wild parties, and riotous living have brought shame to him and his family. Even in a distant country, news travels fast.

But that isn't the worst of it. If only his father would stop grieving...but day after day, without fail, he stands at the door, looking down that dusty road for the younger son's return—longing for him, waiting for him, praying for him.

The older son just can't understand. His father's heart is breaking. His father is being publicly shamed. Why? Why should he want this younger son, this brother of his, to come home?

No. He will not go in!

This younger brother of his deserves to be punished. He has broken the bank. He has broken the Law. He has broken his father's heart.

What the older son, who lacks mercy, does not realize is that even as he judges his younger brother, he is bringing that same judgment back upon himself.

> *Be merciful, just as your Father is merciful. Do not judge, and*
> *you will not be judged. Do not condemn, and you will not be*
> *condemned. Forgive, and you will be forgiven.*
>
> Luke 6:36-37

The younger son embraces the spirit of the world and becomes captive to his own lustful desires, while the older son embraces the spirit of religion and becomes captive to his own pride and self-righteousness.

As Floyd McClung has pointed out, the prodigal is fortunate, very fortunate indeed that his older brother did not meet him first, before his father saw his younger son on the road. As the older son he would have sent the prodigal on his way! There would have been no forgiveness, no celebration, no joyous homecoming!

There's a big difference between being a servant and being a son. If we're a servant, all we can do is bring others to a Master. If we're a son, we can bring them to a Father.

The sad thing about this older son is that though he has everything given to him, he never does anything with his inheritance. He never knows his father's heart or what his father really feels about him.

He's obedient. He works hard. He follows all of the rules, but he acts like a devoted servant instead of a son.

Many of us are like this older son. Though all the Father has is ours, we are not experiencing His fullness in our lives. We are serving Him, night and day, without joy.

I remember the Lord speaking to me once, and saying, "Jack, you're serving Me, but not with joy."

My response was, "Lord, I'm willing to do anything You ask me to do. But to ask me to do it with joy is asking too much."

I didn't realize that I was becoming like this older son. I knew how to serve the Lord, but I didn't have the fullness of joy that is found in His presence, in relationship.

You have made known to me the path of life; you will fill me with joy in your presence, with eternal pleasures at your right hand.

Psalm 16:11

"It's not fair! It's not fair!" this older son is crying. From his perspective, he should be the one to receive the festive robe, the ring, the sandals, and the lavish feast. After all, he has earned it! He has remained in his father's house. He has been the faithful son.

Instead his younger brother receives it all. He becomes the center of attention.

Just a few verses before, Jesus had been sharing the parable of the lost sheep. It's great to be that sheep that is found, but it can be really tough on the ego to be one of the 90 and 9, especially if we're into serving and have not received a revelation of Father's love.

If we don't have relationship, if we don't see ourselves as sons and daughters, what we do for the Lord can become a burden. Like Sue and Lisa, we begin to serve Him out of obligation instead of out of love.

Then before we know it, we are asking ourselves, "Am I a child of God? Does Father really love me?"

I have found people on the mission field who are very much like this older son. When the demands become heavy and the rewards few and far between, they begin to doubt. They cry out to God and say, "Lord, I've done all these things. I've laid down my life. What more do I have to do to be loved?"

> *Come to me, all you who are weary and burdened, and I will give you rest. Take my yoke upon you and learn from me, for I am gentle and humble in heart, and you will find rest for your souls. For my yoke is easy and my burden is light.*
>
> Matthew 11:28-30

When the load is heavy, we're striving. We're trying to impress someone: ourselves, others, perhaps even the Lord.

His yoke is EASY. His burden is LIGHT. When Jesus Christ died on the cross for our sins, He did it all!

> *When he had received the drink, Jesus said, "It is finished." With that, he bowed his head and gave up his spirit.*
>
> John 19:30

"It is finished!" Yes, finished! There is nothing else for us to do but accept the completed work of Calvary and by faith enter into the Sabbath-rest.

> *There remains, then, a Sabbath-rest for the people of God; for anyone who enters God's rest also rests from his own work, just as God did from his.*
>
> Hebrews 4:9-10

Can we rest and work at the same time? Certainly not! Then let's believe the Word of God and lay our burdens down!

Let's stop saying to ourselves and others, "Do, do, do!" when Jesus Christ is so clearly saying in the Scriptures, "Done, done, done!"

The Father wants us to love Him, praise Him, sit in His presence, and share our lives with Him. He's not looking for slaves, but for sons and daughters with whom He can share an intimate relationship.

What do we have to do to be loved? NOTHING. Father does it all! We come. We ask. We receive. Love is a gift, not a reward for service.

Yes, the older son is in his father's house, BUT HE'S LOST. He is just as desperate for love and attention as is his younger brother, but he does not recognize his need.

He Could Never Measure Up

"My father," said Byung Soo, "was a pastor, but he was so legalistic, demanding, and religious that it was almost impossible to live with him. I could never measure up. I know that he believed that he was serving God, but there was never any indication that he knew Him.

"For many years I could not read the Bible. In fact, the only time I heard it read was when I was in church. My father would share passages of Scripture from the pulpit; but even as a pastor, the words sounded so unreal coming from his lips.

"Jack, my father was a hypocrite, plain and simple, and all of his religious mumbo jumbo made me and my brothers nauseous.

"He was so insecure and so controlling that our family lived in fear. Would you believe—my mother was not permitted to leave our home for more than an hour without reporting to him of her whereabouts!

"I felt no love for my father. I tried, but he was always finding fault with what I did. How can you have a relationship, even with God, without love?

"Finally I'd had enough. I turned my back on my family and retreated into the world of street drugs and alcohol.

"Jack, while you were speaking, I was having flashbacks of all the things I've done since I left home. Until we went through the group prayer for cleansing, I had been tormented night and day with pornographic pictures and unclean thoughts."

"I could tell from looking at you, Byung Soo, that much of the oppression had left," I said.

"I've been looking for love all of my life, but I've not found what I've been looking for in drug- and alcohol-induced 'highs,' in pornography, or in immoral relationships. Jack, I want to be free. I want the real thing. No more substitutes."

As we prayed, Byung Soo confessed all of the things that had kept him bound, and Father set him free.

Then I said, "You really need to have a revelation of the Father and His unconditional love for you as His son. He's not like your earthly father, Byung Soo. You were never a son to your own father. Now you need to know what it means to be a son of God!"

As we prayed again, Byung Soo submitted to his Heavenly Father, and Christ became a living presence in his life. For the first time he knew what it was to be a son of God.

"Brother Fred, Is You-All Teachable?"

"Many years ago," said Fred, "when my family and I were living in Wadena, Minnesota, we saw this rattletrap of a three-quarter-ton pickup, with a crudely built camper on the back, pull into our driveway and brake to a halt.

"Out of the pickup came two men. One was an American Indian. The other was a black man. They walked up to the steps of our farmhouse and knocked on the door.

"When I went out to meet them, the sight before me that's etched in my mind and I think forever will be was an unusual one. There stood this Indian, shuffling back n' forth from one foot to the other, and this black man.

"The black man—and he was really black—had the most remarkable white beard and the most engaging smile I think I've ever seen.

"'Is you-all Brother Fred?' he asked.

"'Well, my name is Fred,' I said.

"'Then you-all must be him!'

"'Why are you here?' I asked.

"'Well,' said the black man, 'I was down in the mountains of Kentucky, serving the Lord, when one day God spoke to me and said, "Go to Minnesota and find Brother Fred. I have a message to give you when you meet him."'

"'So I got in my pickup and drove to Minneapolis. When I got there, I began to ask around to see if anybody knew a Brother Fred.

"'Then I came across my Indian friend and he said he knew of a Brother Fred up around the Wadena area that God had been using. So we got into my pickup and here we are.'

"I invited them in. They were such an engaging, such a wonderful pair. They just exuded the love of Christ.

"The black man's name was Bob Sadler. I had never heard of him before, but he was a remarkable man—a man who instinctively, absolutely, and immediately obeyed the leading of the Lord.

"So Bob came in, sat down at the piano, and began to play honky-tonk music. Now I don't like honky-tonk music to begin with, but he played it anyway, and my children sat around the piano absolutely amazed.

"Bob could make that piano jump—literally jump. In fact, there was a vase on top of that piano, and I was afraid that it was going to fall off!

"Bob also had a portable organ that he carried with him. He would take it out of his camper, set it up, and play the most marvelous songs, like 'The Old Rugged Cross' and 'Jesus Is the Sweetest Name I Know.'

"Our children—Juanita, Becky, Daniel, and Scott—were drawn to this man like a magnet to steel.

"Why did God send this unusual messenger to me? Before I answer that question, let me give you a little background.

"The Lord had performed miracles in my life. Just two or three years before, Jesus had set me free from the bondage of mental illness. Then He had brought me back into the ministry, blessing me in a most remarkable way.

"But there was one problem in my home, and that was me. I didn't see it at the time, but I've come to see it since. I wanted to be so right in my walk with God that I had become legalistic.

"I'd been raised in a fundamentalist church, where women were not allowed to wear lipstick and their skirts had to be a certain length. So I demanded that my own daughters wear skirts and dresses to school.

"One night during family council we were discussing this very issue. We had talked about it. Then I said, 'The decision is mine to make. You're not going to wear slacks to school, and that's all there is to it!'

"So my kids stood out in the cold winter of northern Minnesota, in below-zero weather with the wind blowing, waiting for the school bus. They shivered in their dresses because I would not allow them to wear slacks!

"Now I didn't see my decision as being harmful to them at the time. But then I was so busy being right that I couldn't see the wrong in it.

"I remember there was this school picnic, and my daughters asked if they could wear slacks. I absolutely forbid it! So they all went in their dresses.

"Later, as my oldest daughter, Juanita, was playing softball, she deliberately flaunted her dress, flipping it up, just to take advantage of the moment and, I guess, to make me look dumb.

"I loved my children, but I was so imbued with the obsession of not being conformed to this world system that I was strong-willed in my interpretation of what constituted good Christian conduct. I demanded that my children live a certain kind of life as an example of godliness before the world, while I completely failed to see them as individuals with their own unique and special needs.

"This need to be right also was reflected in my ministry, though God continued to bless me in spite of myself.

"Juanita, who was attending junior high school at the time, was one of the first of my children to rebel. From her point of view, what I was preaching from the pulpit was not matching up with my demands of her at home.

"As she told me so, by her words and by her actions, I got even tougher. I didn't want my daughter's disobedience to reflect on the ministry.

"Juanita and I had tremendous battles. I would back her up against the wall and poke my finger into her chest until it actually hurt her. Then I would take her chin in my hands and insist that she listen to what I was saying as she tried to look away.

"Oh, I was hard! It was terrible!

"Well, getting back to Bob Sadler—he was in our home for about two weeks, attending services and touching many lives. Then one day he said, 'Brother Fred, I'm going to walk up that hill.'

"'Why?' I asked.

"'Well, the Lord told me that when I walked to the top of that hill that He would speak to me.'

"So Bob went up the hill, was gone for some time, and came back down again. Then he approached me in the house and said, 'Brother Fred, is you-all teachable?'

"I trembled when Bob said that. How do you respond to someone when they ask, 'Is you-all teachable'?

"I paused and said, 'I think so.'

"Then he said again, 'Brother Fred, is you-all teachable?'

"I said, 'Yes, Bob. I can be taught.'

"'When I got to the top of the hill,' said Bob, 'God spoke to me as to why He had sent me. The Lord has two messages for you, Brother Fred.

"'One concerns your daughter, Juanita. You need to lay hands on her and cast out the spirit of rebellion.'

"Well, that stirred me no end, because I had never prayed for anyone for deliverance of any kind.

"The second thing he said was, 'The Lord wants to do something in you, Brother Fred. You love your children, but you don't know how to show it. You need to ask God to take the hardness out of your heart.'

"When Bob said that, I knew that what he was saying was the truth. So I walked outside, went to the barn, and got before the Lord. Then He began to speak to me about these very things—how I needed His love to flow through me, especially to my children.

"With great weeping I broke before the Lord, asking Him to take this horrible legalism out of my heart—this demand for rightness and godliness which was really not producing any godliness at all.

"I wanted to be so right, so godly, and so holy that I failed to understand that God's holiness always soars on the wings of His love. God is a God of love and He never acts apart from His love, even at the most stringent viewpoint of His holiness.

"That day God did something in my heart. He absolutely revolutionized my spirit and my attitudes about myself, my wife, and my children.

"Over the years I've conducted several family seminars, asking my children to come and share their perspective of our parenting in their lives. Juanita, in recounting this experience, said something I felt was quite insightful.

"She said: 'As long as my father was so right, I could resist him. But when I found out that he really loved me, I couldn't resist him anymore.'

"How true that is!

"It's a marvelous work of God's grace to be transformed from the deadness of orthodoxy into the genuine life of the love of the Father!

"This was dramatically brought to my attention several years later when my son, Daniel, came to me and said:

"'Dad, I just want to tell you something. I really respect you and I love you.'

"I said, 'What brought that on?'

"'Well,' he said, 'I just wanted to tell you that.'

"'Why do you respect me?' I asked.

"'Dad, I not only respect you, but I trust you. The reason for that is this: I really can't trust someone that's always right, but I know I can trust someone who is willing to be wrong.'

"That said mountains to me at the time. What a tribute to the change that God had worked in my heart!

"Bob Sadler,[5] who was born a slave and raised as a child by his grandmother, later married and settled in Ohio. He spent many years traveling throughout the United States and Canada, blessing God's people and edifying the church of Jesus Christ.

"How thankful I am for that humble, beautiful man who, at the Lord's leading, was willing to leave the mountains of Kentucky and come all the way to Wadena, Minnesota.

"Bob brought me out of my legalistic preaching, parenting, and living into a life of simply letting the Father's love flow through me—first to my wife and my children, then to the church and the world."

God is not interested in our good works or our rules. There is nothing we can do, nothing we can offer Him as a Holy God that He can accept— except our faith in Jesus Christ.

Chapter Eight

Under the Law

*The older brother became angry and refused to go in. So his
father went out and pleaded with him. But he answered his
father, "Look! All these years I've been slaving for you and
never disobeyed your orders. Yet you never gave me even a
young goat so I could celebrate with my friends."*

Luke 15:28-29

Dedicated service. Unfailing obedience. Sounds good, doesn't
it?

As Christian parents, many of us would be pleased to have a son who,
like this older brother in Luke's parable, stays at home, works hard, and
does whatever his father tells him to do!

But in the Kingdom of God, it's not what we do, but what Christ does
in and through us that brings joy to the heart of the Father!

Is our focus on Christ—what He has done on the cross, what He is
doing in our lives? Or is our focus on ourselves—what we have done,
what we are doing?

For the Pharisees, who are zealous in their interpretation and performance of Old Testament Law, it is the latter.

*Everything they do is done for men to see: They make their phy-
lacteries wide and the tassels on their garments long; they love
the place of honor at banquets and the most important seats in*

> *the synagogues; they love to be greeted in the marketplaces and*
> *to have men call them "Rabbi."*
>
> Matthew 23:5-7

But Jesus is not impressed. He is not interested in the sect's emphasis on performance or its rigid adherence to details. Both fall short of the true meaning of Old Testament Law.

> *Woe to you Pharisees, because you give God a tenth of your*
> *mint, rue and all other kinds of garden herbs, but you neglect*
> *justice and the love of God. You should have practiced the latter*
> *without leaving the former undone.*
>
> Luke 11:42

Holiness, as Jesus shares in this passage and in Matthew 23:23, is a commitment to justice, mercy, and faithfulness which goes beyond mere adherence to ritual observance. While true spirituality would require the Pharisees to love the very men they hold in such contempt, the tax collectors and the "sinners."

But an even greater condemnation awaits these religious leaders for their misuse of the Word of God.

> *"These people honor me with their lips, but their hearts are far*
> *from me. They worship me in vain; their teachings are but rules*
> *taught by men." You have let go of the commands of God and*
> *are holding on to the traditions of men.*
>
> Mark 7:6b-8

The problem is not one of doctrine. On basic doctrinal issues, Jesus has sided with the Pharisees openly before the crowds. It is the oral traditions that they hold as authoritative and binding that are nullifying the Word of God and making Old Testament Law, which is already more than most Jewish people can bear, even more complex.

These oral traditions, which are interpretations or teachings that have been given by thousands of rabbis, have been handed down by former generations and are being used by the Pharisees to define and interpret the Law of Moses. Why? So that no man will transgress the Law in ignorance!

That is why so much of what Jesus is sharing in this parable of the prodigal son is so radical, so life-changing. He is openly challenging the religious leaders' understanding of the intent of the Law.

In their strict and rigid adherence to Mosaic Law, the Pharisees have become legalistic. They are presenting an approach to serving God—rules, rules, and more rules—that is causing many Jews to rebel and turn their backs in despair.

What about us, as the body of Christ? Are we misusing or adding to the Word of God? Are we allowing the traditions of men to ensnare us in the complex web of legalism?

We are if we rely on our good works as a means to salvation or spiritual growth. We are if we insist that others follow a certain list of rules to be accepted within our Christian community.

God is not interested in our good works or our rules. There is nothing we can do, nothing we can offer Him as a Holy God that He can accept—except our faith in Jesus Christ.

Has someone told us that we need to be baptized, join the church, take Holy Communion, teach a Sunday school class, feed the poor, or donate large sums of money to religious charities to inherit eternal life?

This is legalism. Nowhere in the Word of God does it tell us we have to do any of these things.

> *For it is by grace you have been saved, through faith—and this not from yourselves, it is the gift of God—not by works, so that no one can boast.*
>
> Ephesians 2:8-9

Salvation is by the grace of God, through faith. It has nothing to do with good works.

All we have to do is acknowledge our need as sinners and accept Jesus into our life as Lord and Savior. Even the faith that is needed is a gift of God!

Has someone told us that if we want to mature in Christ we need to read our Bibles, fast, pray, win souls, memorize Scripture, attend church faithfully, and tithe?

This, too, is legalism. To be sure, all of these things have their place in a Christian's daily walk with the Lord. But when someone tries to give us a list of rules or guidelines in terms of how many hours we should spend in Bible study and prayer, how many verses of Scripture we should memorize, or how many souls we should win for Christ, beware!

If we fail to measure up—and most of us will—we will feel guilty. If we fail more often than we succeed, we will give up in despair.

It's God's grace and the Holy Spirit in us that will bring us to maturity in Christ, not human effort or faithful adherence to a set of procedures.

Has someone told us we must give up alcohol, tobacco, movies, playing cards, popular music, comic books, or certain types of food if we want to be accepted as a church member in good standing? Or as women that we are never to wear slacks, sleeveless blouses, makeup, short hair, or skirts that are not at least one inch below the knee?

This, too, is legalism. When we try to create an arbitrary standard for Christian conduct, we are misusing the Word of God. We are placing the focus on ourselves—what we do or don't do—instead of on the Lord Jesus Christ!

Facing a similar challenge when Jewish Christians are insisting that Gentile converts adopt Jewish customs and observe the Law of Moses, the Apostle Paul writes:

> *You foolish Galatians! Who has bewitched you? Before your*
> *very eyes Jesus Christ was clearly portrayed as crucified. I*
> *would like to learn just one thing from you: Did you receive the*
> *Spirit by observing the law, or by believing what you heard?*
> *Are you so foolish? After beginning with the Spirit, are you now*
> *trying to attain your goal by human effort?*
>
> Galatians 3:1-3

Are we trying to obtain our goal by human effort? Or by believing what we have heard from the Word of God?

Do we see the Bible as a list of commands? Or as a book of promises? Legalism, or the letter of the Law, kills. But the Spirit gives life!

Remember the throne of God—that 24-hour full-service grace station where all we have to do is say, "Fill 'er up" and Father, the Chief Mechanic, does it all?

Well, for those of us who feel we must work hard and pay for what we get, there's another option: The Pit Stop.

Just down the road, last building on the right, The Pit—as it is called by its less than satisfied customers—is a 24-hour self-service gas station that offers a do-it-yourself car wash and a nine-to-five auto service, by appointment only.

Almost everyone in Certain County, U.S.A. goes there, from Uncle Ted to Grandma Ann, lured in the door by the specials that appear in the Hellsgate door-to-door flyer. This week's coupon for a free quart of milk and a 12-point oil change—all for only $15.95—has been so popular that sole owner, Stan Devile, has had to leave the front office to his secretary, Leigh Galistic, just to meet the demand for Serpentine air filters in the back bay!

Tom Tradition, the firm's customer service representative, answers phones, schedules appointments, and handles all complaints. He knows from years of experience that the best answer is usually no answer at all.

When a customer questions an estimate, finds the work less than satisfactory, or quibbles over the final bill, Tom gives a meaningful pause, breaks forth in a smile, and says: "Thanks for bringing that to our attention. But as you can see, we've been serving the good customers of Certain County for over 40 years and that's how we've always done it!"

Harold Holier-than-Thou, chief mechanic, supervises the maintenance crew: Frank Faultfinder, Rufus Rule, Lester Law, and intern-in-training Stephen Self-Righteous. His technical assistant, Farah See, handles the back office, where she files invoices, inventories parts, and orders lubricants.

A most unique operation, this nine-to-five auto service offers a 30-minute verbal guarantee on all parts and labor. But as many will tell you in confidence, and others in graphic horror, the crew promises little and delivers even less!

Frank Faultfinder, senior mechanic, is the analyst-in-residence. When no one else can see the need for timely maintenance, Frank can. It is his sole responsibility to go over every auto, van, and truck with a fine-tooth comb, looking for possible defects.

In his 40 years of experience, Frank has never seen a car that didn't need at least $400 in repairs—even a new model, fresh off the assembly line. "They just don't make them like they used to," he says with a smile.

Lester Law and Rufus Rule are Frank's right-hand men. They do the actual repairs. Seasoned mechanics, they know the ins and outs of foreign and domestic maintenance, from procedure to final billing. Nothing—believe me, nothing—takes them by surprise.

As Lester and Rufus are quick to point out, should any customer dare to ask, for every procedure there is a right way and a wrong way to do the job. And the right way is always by the book!

Now let's be honest. What, as sons and daughters of the living God, would draw us to this legalistic gas station? Convenience? The opportunity to do it ourselves?

Do we need to see ourselves as condemned, always in need of repair? Or pay dearly for something that is already ours in Christ?

When we allow ourselves to get caught up in the constraints of the Law, we, too, will find ourselves involved in an approach to the Christian life that, like the maintenance crew at The Pit Stop, promises little and delivers even less.

When Jesus laid down His life on the cross, He said: "It is finished!" The penalty, the demands of the Law, have been met once and for all. Praise God!

Let's recognize The Pit Stop for what it is: a counterfeit version of The Grace Station, straight from the pit of hell!

As sons and daughters of our Heavenly Father, we don't need an appointment. We don't need to do it ourselves. We don't even need to submit ourselves to the legalistic demands of Harold Holier-than-Thou and his motley crew!

Let's claim and appropriate what is already ours in Christ! Let's come boldly to the throne of grace and ask the Father to fill us up!

"It's Your Fault I Got Sick!"

"I had heard that Jack Winter was coming to our church in Hamilton, Ontario," said Richard, "to hold a week-long seminar on *The Father Heart of God* and forgiveness. Knowing that I had a problem with holding grudges against people and not being able to forgive, I decided to attend.

"The person I really wanted to forgive was my sister, Maria. We had gotten along well when we were younger, but had begun to drift apart in our late teens, early twenties.

"Maria was a gossip, something she could have picked up at our old church. She would look down on others, talk behind their back, and say hurtful things. She also had a bad temper and experienced mood swings.

"Things got worse when I met my future wife, Elizabeth. Then Maria began to say cruel things about both of us. She did congratulate us on our engagement, but then she told everyone else, including my parents, that we wouldn't make it, were too stupid, were too young, etc.

"I forgave Maria once, but she continued to share her cruel gossip with anyone who would stop and listen.

"My parents gave us a wonderful wedding, but Elizabeth and I never really felt their hearts were in it. Maria even had the audacity to say things behind our backs on our wedding day!

"After the ceremony, my wife and I decided that we would have nothing to do with Maria again. I could almost say that at that point I hated her. I just couldn't believe that my own sister would be that cruel.

"Our decision to end any relationship I had with Maria really tore the family apart. Then about a year later she was married. Both my wife and I went to Maria's wedding, but after that we never saw her or her husband or visited in their home.

"If there were any holidays or family get-togethers, my wife and I would go on the day after to avoid any contact with Maria. For over eight years we lived this way, doing our best to avoid her.

"Once Maria ran into me while I was working in a store and asked how I was doing. (She knew she had taken a chance by talking to me.) Then she asked me if I would forgive her.

"I told her to her face that I didn't think I could. Then she walked away, doing her best to hold back the tears.

"All of this conflict was making me extremely ill. If I even saw Maria on the street, I would look the other way, pretend she wasn't there, or quickly duck out of sight.

"I was waiting for Maria to confess everything that she had done wrong to me and my wife. But Maria kept acting as if she had absolutely no clue as to why we were angry with her. This made me even more furious!

"My family kept encouraging me to forgive Maria, but I would say, 'No way! Never! She hurt us. We haven't done anything wrong.

"'I'm sick and tired of looking like I'm the bad guy and having her blame my wife for the separation between us as brother and sister.

"'When Maria comes and admits what she has done and how much she has hurt us, then we will think about forgiving her. Not before.'

"Jack's series on *The Father Heart of God* began Sunday evening. I had explained the conflict I had with my sister to a friend, and each night before the meeting began, Melissa would ask me if I had called Maria. I said, 'No.' (Though one night I did try to call her, but changed my mind and turned away.)

"On Wednesday Jack had everyone in the audience stand. Then he led us in a group prayer to forgive those who had hurt us, especially our family members, beginning with our fathers, mothers, brothers, and sisters.

"I had my eyes closed when I heard Jack say the word *sister*. Then I stopped.

"I could not do it! I could not forgive my sister, Maria, for all the trouble she had caused my wife and me.

"Jack asked Pam, a member of his ministry team, to come over and help me pray. 'Richard,' she said, 'can you forgive your sister?'

"'No,' I said, my eyes tightly closed and my arms folded close to my chest.

"'Can I take your sister's place?' she said. I agreed.

"'Richard,' said Pam, standing in as Maria, 'I'm sorry for all the things I said about you and your wife. I know my words hurt you deeply.

It was wrong of me to think, let alone say what I did to you and others. Please forgive me. I was just hurting myself.'

"I thought, 'What nerve she has to ask for my forgiveness.' Then I had to do everything I could think of to stop myself from hitting her.

"But Pam kept talking, asking me to forgive her. Finally I said, 'No. I can't do it on my own,' and began to cry.

"'Richard,' she said, 'none of us can do it on our own. We all need God's help. Let's pray and ask Him to give you a spirit of forgiveness.'

"'Okay,' I said. I knew Pam was right. I really needed God's help.

"So Pam put her arms around me and prayed that the Holy Spirit would come upon me. Then everything that had been brewing inside of me began to spew forth like red-hot lava from a smoldering volcano.

"I began to yell at Pam, striking her back with my clenched fists. 'I hate you! I hate you! I hate you! How could you do this to me?

"'I'm your only brother. How could you say such cruel things? How could you break my heart?

"'It's your fault I got sick with ulcerative colitis and finally had to have surgery. Now I'll have to wear this bag for the rest of my life!'

"In those few minutes it all came out—the anger, pain, and hatred that I had been feeling for over eight years. I had blamed Maria, my parents, my friends, and even my own wife for everything.

"I cried in Pam's arms. I let it all come out.

"Finally Jack came over and said, 'Richard, are you okay?'

"'Yeah,' I said. I felt calm. There was a peace inside of me, as if something had been released.

"When I came to the meetings on Friday evening, Melissa said, 'Richard, have you called Maria?'

"'No,' I said, 'but I will.'

"Sunday morning came. Melissa asked again, 'Richard, have you called Maria?'

"'No,' I said, 'but I will.'

"That evening I told my wife what I was going to do and she agreed. I sat down by the phone and asked God to prepare my sister's and my own heart for what I was about to say.

"It was about 9 P.M. when I called Maria, and we talked for almost three hours! I explained everything to her in detail—how I had received Jesus as my Lord and Savior and then about what had happened during Jack's seminar.

"I told her to thank God, not me, for my calling her, because I could never have done it in my own strength.

"That night I forgave my sister. Maria said it was the happiest night of her life and that she would mark it down on her calendar. Then she began to share the troubles she'd had and how God had been trying to get a hold of her life.

"Now we do things as a family again and the healing continues.

"In a few minutes the Holy Spirit released me from eight years of bitterness, hatred, judgment, and unforgiveness. Then the Father came and gave me His love and His heart.

"I came away from that call expecting nothing from Maria, even though she apologized to me over the phone. All of what was said and done had been forgiven.

"Now both my wife and I are free to love again. It's unbelievable. Thanks be to God!"

"Why Is There No Grace for Me?"

"I had the opportunity to hear Jack on tape," said Dennis, "before I met him in person. We had a couple in our church who had just come back from Youth With A Mission, and they had secured a set of Jack's *Father Heart of God* tapes through their Discipleship Training School.

"One day as I was out taking a walk, listening to Jack's tape on 'Releasing Hurts Through Forgiveness,' I was suddenly in the Spirit and began to feel this large stack of IOU's in my back pocket.

"I knew that the Word teaches us to forgive or we will not be forgiven.

Do not judge, and you will not be judged. Do not condemn, and you will not be condemned. Forgive, and you will be forgiven.
Luke 6:37

I also knew that I had forgiven the people who down through the years I felt had wronged me. But God was showing me that, like the unmerciful servant in Jesus' parable (Matt. 18:21-35), I had not forgiven the debt.

"God says there were two trees in the Garden of Eden (Genesis 2:9,16-17). One was the Tree of Life—that's Jesus! The other was the Tree of the Knowledge of Good and Evil.

"Many of us go to the Tree of the Knowledge of Good and Evil daily and eat. We weigh the rights and the wrongs, judging others based on what they've done. That kind of thinking leads to death.

"That was the tree at which I had been eating. A number of people had wronged me down through the years, and I had kept a very complete record of those wrongs.

"Suddenly I realized that this was not the way that God wanted me to live. This was not the love of Christ flowing through me. It says in the Word:

> *It [love] is not rude, it is not self-seeking, it is not easily*
> *angered, it keeps no record of wrongs.*
>
> 1 Corinthians 13:5

"If we eat at the Tree of the Knowledge of Good and Evil, we will find it very difficult to forgive. If we eat at the Tree of Life (i.e., Jesus), we will find His love enabling us to forgive.

"So I recognized that I had this huge stack of IOU's in my back pocket, and as I continued on my walk that afternoon, God reminded me of the people who had wronged me. As each person's name came to my mind, one by one I tore up the IOU's.

"Unforgiveness was a stronghold that had kept me bound for many years. As I walked, liberty came to my spirit and I felt the presence of the Lord. It was marvelous and I was really blessed!

"Another day, as I was listening to one of Jack's tapes on forgiveness, I again found myself in the Spirit. This time I was experiencing an open vision when the thought came to me, 'Agree with your adversary quickly.'

> *Settle matters quickly with your adversary who is taking you to*
> *court. Do it while you are still with him on the way, or he may*
> *hand you over to the judge, and the judge may hand you over to*
> *the officer, and you may be thrown into prison. I tell you the*
> *truth, you will not get out until you have paid the last penny.*
>
> Matthew 5:25-26

"I saw myself sitting in the witness stand of a courtroom, being badgered by a team of prosecuting attorneys. They would take turns coming at me with all kinds of accusations.

"Then they would take what I said and twist it, malign it, and throw it back at me. These attorneys were unrelenting in their prosecution.

"As I was attempting to answer their accusations, I would quote the Word of God and try to explain why I had done certain things. But seemingly unmoved, they did not cease their attack.

"As one of the attorneys would become weary, he would sit down. Then another would take his place. It didn't seem to matter what I said or how I responded, the accusations kept coming at me like the rapid fire of a machine gun.

"I began to weep. I knew that I could not go on this way.

"As I watched the vision unfold, I began to realize that in a very real sense that this was what I had been going through in my own life. I had been under attack because I had been reaping what I had sown.

"Then I began to cry out to God: 'Why is there no grace for me?'

"From over my right shoulder, in real life, came a trumpet voice, saying: 'Judge not, lest ye be judged. For in the same measure you mete, it will be meted back to you again.'

"Suddenly it was as though a light had been turned on. I saw how I had been living a life of judgment towards my family, my brothers and sisters in Christ, and the world.

"The birthright that had been handed to me by my parents and that I had grown up with through the church was one of judgment. I had become like one of the Pharisees, praying, 'I thank you, God, that I am not as other men.' I should have been praying, 'Be merciful to me, a sinner.'

"I had judged many in the body of Christ, both individuals and entire denominations, for what I thought was wrong doctrine.

"So I went back to my childhood and, the best I could remember, I began to release teachers, family members, relatives, friends, denominations, ministries, and TV evangelists—anyone that I had ever judged.

"Then I returned to the open vision of the courtroom. Again I was in the witness stand. But this time the judge turned to me and said, 'Dennis, you may step down.'

"Finally! The trial was over! The verdict was in. The prosecuting attorneys had been silenced.

"I felt like a ten-ton weight had been lifted off my shoulders. It was like a conversion experience to walk in the grace of God as a free man!

"A few days later I saw fireworks going off in the Spirit as I realized that each and every person that I had forgiven had been released!"

Both sons are lost—one with an empty stomach, the other with an empty heart. Both need the love of their father. Both need to come home.

Chapter Nine

The Offense

*But he answered his father, "Look! All these years I've been
slaving for you and never disobeyed your orders. Yet you never
gave me even a young goat so I could celebrate with my
friends. But when this son of yours who has squandered your
property with prostitutes comes home, you kill the fattened calf
for him!"*

Luke 15:29-30

*R*ichard was as offended by Maria's words of judgment as was
the older son by his father's party for the returning prodigal.
It's easy to be caught in the snare of pride, especially when the enemy of
our souls is so eager to see us fall into sin.

On the surface, this older son's response to his father's invitation
could seem almost ludicrous. When his father divided the family estate, as
firstborn he received the larger portion, or about two-thirds.

So he has all the resources he needs to celebrate. Why hasn't he used
them?

But the issue here is not a young goat or even a party complete with
barbecued beef! What is inciting this older son's wrath is the relationship
and love his younger brother is experiencing with their father, in spite of
his past sin and disobedience, and it's just not fair!

Life does not work this way. Can't his father understand? The Law is
very clear as to the judgment that must be made regarding this type of sin.
The men of the community should be stoning this prodigal son of his, not
celebrating his return!

All these years, as the elder son, he has slaved for his father, never disobeying a single one of his orders. He has stayed at home, faithfully working in the fields and managing the estate, and what has it gotten him?

But this older son is not the only one who is offended. The Pharisees are furious. The first two parables may have been open to interpretation. But this one is, without a doubt, a definite attack on their way of life and their interpretation of the intent of the Law.

It is blasphemy! What gives Jesus the right to humiliate them, the religious leaders of the day, when He Himself is so willing to receive and eat with "the sinners," the tax collectors, and the misfits among them?

Oh, how difficult it is for the Pharisees to receive Jesus' correction when they are so absolutely certain that they are right! How easy it is for them to condemn Him, not realizing that they are the ones who by their own pride have become caught in an offense.

But the fact remains that, like the older son, the Pharisees have been depending on their own good works and strict adherence to the Law to make them righteous before a Holy God. Now Jesus is telling them it just isn't going to work. It isn't going to earn them eternal life.

What then shall we say? That the Gentiles, who did not pursue
righteousness, have obtained it, a righteousness that is by faith;
but Israel, who pursued a law of righteousness, has not attained
it. Why not? Because they pursued it not by faith but as if it
were by works. They stumbled over the "stumbling stone"
[Jesus Christ].

Romans 9:30-32

The Pharisees have put the cart before the horse. Jesus is saying that relationship, not religion, is the key. When they get their hearts right before God, then good works and obedience will flow naturally out of a heart of love for the Father and all that He has created.

One of them, an expert in the law, tested him with this question:
"Teacher, which is the greatest commandment in the Law?"
Jesus replied: "Love the Lord your God with all your heart and
with all your soul and with all your mind. This is the first and
greatest commandment. And the second is like it: 'Love your
neighbor as yourself.' All the Law and the Prophets hang on
these two commandments."

Matthew 22:35-40

What happens when this older son is offended? He becomes angry and begins to lash out at his father, accusing him of the unjust treatment he is receiving as a faithful son compared to his disobedient brother.

Now anger is an emotion that God has given us and, when used appropriately, is meant for our good. But it is always to be directed against evil, not the evildoer, and it is always to be kept in balance by God's love, compassion, and mercy.

That is not what is happening here. The older son not only hates his brother's sin, but also in anger he totally disowns him, calling him *"this son of yours"* (v. 30). There is no love, compassion, or mercy in his heart for the sinner. Only a desperate need to bring his younger brother to justice!

As a destructive emotion, hatred flows from man's sinful nature.

The acts of the sinful nature are obvious: sexual immorality, impurity and debauchery; idolatry and witchcraft; hatred, discord, jealousy, fits of rage, selfish ambition, dissensions, factions and envy; drunkenness, orgies, and the like. I warn you, as I did before, that those who live like this will not inherit the kingdom of God.

Galatians 5:19-21

But as we can see from this passage in Galatians, the sin of hatred is no better nor is it any worse in the eyes of God than any other sin, including those supposedly committed by the prodigal son.

The second thing that happens when this older brother is offended is that he begins to judge not only the character, but also the sin of his younger brother; and in so doing, he forces his earthly and his Heavenly Father to judge him as well.

Do not judge, or you too will be judged. For in the same way you judge others, you will be judged, and with the measure you use, it will be measured to you.

Matthew 7:1-2

Judgment is a serious matter. As sons and daughters of the living God, it can force us to take our place on the witness stand where the accuser of the brethren, Satan himself, prosecutes us unmercifully. Or, like Dennis, it can keep us bound in a debtor's prison with those for whom we are unwilling to forgive the debt (Matthew 18:21-35).

Even the Father does not judge us. What makes us feel that we are qualified to keep another bound hand and foot by our own judgments and our unwillingness to forgive?

Moreover, the Father judges no one, but has entrusted all judgment to the Son.

John 5:22

For if you forgive men when they sin against you, your heavenly Father will also forgive you. But if you do not forgive men their sins, your Father will not forgive your sins.

Matthew 6:14-15

Unforgiveness will harden our hearts. If we have really forgiven someone, we will be tenderhearted toward that person.

The third thing that happens when this older brother is offended is that he begins to play "the blame game." After all, it is his father's fault that he, as the older son, is angry and unwilling to join in the celebration. Or is it?

How many of us have judged our Heavenly Father when things have not gone the way we had planned? Job, who suffered far more than any of us will ever suffer at any one point in our lives, indulged in this luxury and was firmly rebuked by the Sovereign Lord Himself (Job 38–41).

God's ways are not our ways. We may never understand His purposes, but we can trust Him, knowing that He loves us and is working on our behalf.

And we know that in all things God works for the good of those who love him, who have been called according to his purpose.

Romans 8:28

This is submission, yielding our very lives to the Father. It is an act of trust, our way of saying we are accountable to God. Then we accept His will for our lives, knowing that in His perfect love He will always give us His very best.

In this case, the older son reverses the role. He demands that his father become accountable to him and explain his actions, thereby calling into question his father's love for him as a son and his willingness to always give him his best.

The fourth thing thing that happens when this older son is offended is that he condemns himself. By the words of his own mouth, he tears off the mask and exposes himself for what he really is: a son who has been good for all the wrong reasons, a son who does not know how to love or be loved.

One day, as Jesus was healing a demon-possessed man who was both blind and mute, the Pharisees accused Him of driving out the demons by the authority of Beelzebub, the prince of demons. To this accusation, Jesus replied:

> *You brood of vipers, how can you who are evil say anything*
> *good? For out of the overflow of the heart the mouth speaks.*
> *The good man brings good things out of the good stored up in*
> *him, and the evil man brings evil things out of the evil stored up*
> *in him.*
>
> Matthew 12:34-35

Like the Pharisees and this older son, we may be able to deceive ourselves and others by our outward appearance. But the minute we open our mouths and speak, the show is over and the truth is revealed for all to see.

Father is not only concerned with what we do. He is also concerned with what we feel and think (our attitudes and motives).

The older son is zealous in his desire to do what is right, but his heart condemns him. He is bitter, unmerciful, self-righteous, and proud. In many ways, he is in worse shape than is his younger brother.

The last thing that happens when this older son is offended is that he isolates himself by rejecting the very person who could truly meet his need: his father. Even when his father goes the extra mile and leaves the party to plead with him to join the celebration, the older son only responds in anger.

How are we, as brothers and sisters in Christ, to respond when offenses come? Jesus said:

> *But I tell you who hear me: Love your enemies, do good to*
> *those who hate you, bless those who curse you, pray for those*
> *who mistreat you.*
>
> Luke 6:27-28

What is the missing ingredient? Why does this parable seem to end with no resolution? Does the older son ever join the party?

Pride is the hindrance that keeps this older son bound. Only humility and the willingness to say like the prodigal, "Father I have sinned against heaven and against you" can ever set him free. Until then he is hopelessly enmeshed in his own emotional downward spiral of anger, judgment, blame, condemnation, isolation, and rejection that can only lead to more misery, pain, and ultimately, death.

If we condemn, we'll be condemned. If we forgive, we'll be forgiven.

The Father's heart, the Father's desire for each of us, is that we love ourselves and others as He has loved us. In fact, that is why Jesus has been sharing the three parables in Luke 15. He is describing His Father's limitless love for the sinner who repents.

The younger son has no boundaries, while the older son builds walls. The younger son physically separates himself from his father and leaves home, while the older son emotionally separates himself from his father and stays in his father's house.

Both sons are lost—one with an empty stomach, the other with an empty heart. Both need the love of their father. Both need to come home.

Secure in Papa God

"My alcoholic father left when my mother was pregnant with me," said Arlene. "I didn't see him more than four or five times after that.

"But when I was eight, my father did come to visit, and with him was another woman and another eight-year-old girl!

"Any fantasies I'd had up until that time about having a place in my father's heart were shattered. I felt replaced by that other little girl.

"I was so upset and so angry that I told my father that I never wanted to see him again! And I didn't—until I was 18 years old.

"The male relatives in my life were rather weak and fractured people. As I look back, men were not able to protect me, provide for me, or affirm me.

"My mother worked very hard to support us. One time when my father was visiting, he gave me a five-dollar bill—as if that would make up for all the years of nonsupport. I was so upset, I threw the money back at him.

"Early on in life I received the message that men could not take care of me. So I decided then and there that I needed to take care of myself.

"Throughout my childhood I went to Christian schools. My mother and my aunties, I'm sure, prayed for me.

"I always loved Jesus, but I think I was a little afraid of God as Father. Like my own father, I was afraid that He might punish or abandon me.

"Through listening to some cassettes by Jack Winter on *The Father Heart of God*, I became aware that something was missing. I had never had a meaningful relationship with one of the most important people in my life: my father.

"Later, as Jack and I met and discussed the content of the tapes, I began to understand that God wanted to be that father that I had never known as a little child. He wanted to love me, care for me, protect me, affirm me—do everything my own father had not been able to do.

"When Jack and I began to pray, I discovered I had a lot of fear and resistance to receiving the Father's love. 'Can I open myself up to trust a father, even God?' I asked. 'Will He really be there for me? If I allow myself to become vulnerable, will I be hurt again, displaced, cast aside, left alone?'

"As Father's love began to penetrate the seemingly impenetrable walls of distrust that I had built over the years, I knew I had to face my fear of allowing Him total access to my heart. Tears began to flow as I decided to release my pain and my disillusionment.

"Suddenly, deep from within, I burst out, 'I be! I be! I be! I be different.'

"When I left that day, I knew in my heart that I was going to live this new life as a different being.

"As time has gone on, I've felt the Father's hand on my life. When I am with Him I feel delight, joy, and peace.

"His presence seems to be there at all times and my roots have become divine roots. I know that I am truly safe and secure in Papa God.

"As I cultivate a life of close communion with the Father, I am experiencing the power of His healing love. I have needed consistent proofs of that love and His commitment and He, in His tenderness, has responded.

"Father has given me a new identity. I, Arlene, am His daughter!"

A Wagon Full of Toys

I was ministering to about 40 men, most of whom had served their time in prison or the penitentiary and were now involved in a Christian re-entry program run by Teen Challenge. I was telling them that they were part of the Lazarus generation that God is raising up.

"You were so dead," I said, "you stunk. Even your mother had given up on you.

"But God is not the God of funerals. He's the God of resurrection! He has raised you from the dead, and now I have come to take off your grave clothes!

"Your problem is not drugs, or alcohol, or even the criminal activity in which you've been involved. Your real problem is that you have never received the right kind of love."

As I looked over the group, my eyes fell on Mike. Full of rejection, like a porcupine, no one could even begin to get close to him.

Later, when as a group we were praying to forgive our fathers for any hurts they may have caused us, Mike had a pained look on his face. So one of the men on staff went over, put his hand on Mike's shoulder, and began to help him pray through to forgiveness.

Standing in front of the group, I could see Mike's countenance change. I was curious. What had happened?

Afterwards Mike said, "The reason I hated my father so much was because he would buy gifts for my sisters, but he would never buy one for me.

"I didn't realize," said Mike, "how deep my anger was until we began to pray together as a group to forgive our fathers. I couldn't do it. There was just too much pain inside of me.

"Then Bill came over and put his arm around my shoulder. As we prayed, I sensed God giving me the willingness and the emotional release that I needed.

"Then something truly amazing happened. I saw my Heavenly Father walking towards me with a wagon full of toys! I just couldn't believe it."

Later, as the Lord began to move within the group, Mike cried out to God to forgive him for the ways in which he had rejected and emotionally wounded his wife and children.

Then, as we finished, one by one the men began to go to Mike, sharing words of affirmation and love. Once a porcupine, now Mike gladly accepted their hugs and hugged them in return.

Yes, the Father knew just what was needed, as that day, through prayer and a wagon full of toys, He set Mike free!

*We can be at home with God. We can
kick off our shoes, relax, and just be ourselves.
We can even make mistakes.*

Chapter Ten

In His Presence

*"My son," the father said, "you are always with me, and every-
thing I have is yours."*

Luke 15:31

No matter what kind of mansion or dwelling place your father
has, if you don't know that you have a place in his heart, you
will never feel at home. Like Arlene, Mike, and the older son, you will
always be searching for a way to belong.

But when you know that you have a place in your father's heart and
you experience the love that he has for you as his child, then what's his is
yours. Love makes it that way!

One day I met a young man at a Teen Challenge Center in Ontario.
When he was eight years old, he had come home from school, only to find
that both of his parents had left—totally abandoned him. Since then he
had lived in 40 different foster homes.

When he was in his early teens, a pastor had led him to the Lord. Then
for 12 years that same pastor had sexually abused him.

This young man was so full of anger and bitterness that when we
prayed as a group to forgive those people who had hurt us, he was unable
to pray. So as a team we had to minister to him privately.

This young man had never known a safe place, a place he could call
home.

How many of us can identify with him? How many of us have grown
up in a dysfunctional family where Mom was an alcoholic, or Dad sexually abused us, or both parents were threatening to file for divorce? With
so much fear and insecurity in our lives, home has not been a safe place.

Abandonment is the deepest, most painful type of rejection that a person can ever experience. Even Jesus Himself could hardly bear it when His disciples abandoned Him and the Father had to turn His back, as He bore the sins of the world on the cross.

> *At the sixth hour darkness came over the whole land until the*
> *ninth hour. And at the ninth hour Jesus cried out in a loud*
> *voice, "Eloi, Eloi, lama sabachthani?"—which means, "My*
> *God, my God, why have you forsaken me?"*
>
> Mark 15:33-34

So knowing that He will soon leave this world to go and be with His Father, Jesus is trying to comfort His disciples as they meet in the Upper Room to share the Passover meal. He wants them to know that no matter what happens in the days to come, He is not abandoning them and He will come again!

> *Do not let your hearts be troubled. Trust in God; trust also in*
> *me. In my Father's house are many rooms; if it were not so, I*
> *would have told you. I am going there to prepare a place for*
> *you. And if I go and prepare a place for you, I will come back*
> *and take you to be with me that you also may be where I am.*
>
> John 14:1-3

Now this illustration has special significance for the disciples, for it clearly refers to the marriage customs observed by a Jewish bridegroom and his bride. What is confusing is that it refers to the church, a mystery yet to be revealed, and to a place that is as yet unknown to them.

By using the illustration, Jesus is saying that His Father has chosen a bride for Him (the church) and in a few days will send His promise or seal (the Holy Spirit) of the betrothal.

> *And you also were included in Christ when you heard the*
> *word of truth, the gospel of your salvation. Having believed,*
> *you were marked in him with a seal, the promised Holy Spirit,*
> *who is a deposit guaranteeing our inheritance until the redemp-*
> *tion of those who are God's possession—to the praise of his*
> *glory.*
>
> Ephesians 1:13-14

But first the bride must be redeemed. This Jesus will do by His death on the cross and His resurrection from the dead. Like Boaz did for Ruth in the Old Testament (Ruth 4:1-12), He will step forward as a kinsman-redeemer to buy back the inheritance that has been lost through the entrance of sin into the world by one man (Adam).

Then while His bride is preparing herself for the marriage feast, as Paul alludes to in his epistle to the church at Corinth,

> *I am jealous for you with a godly jealousy. I promised you to one husband, to Christ, so that I might present you as a pure virgin to him.*
>
> 2 Corinthians 11:2

Jesus will ascend to heaven. There He will be in His Father's house, as was the custom of the times, adding on or preparing the additional room(s) for His bride.

Finally, when everything is ready, He will come again! Then He will take His bride with Him, so where He is, she can be also—and the marriage feast of the Lamb will begin!

But until then, Jesus says:

> *I will not leave you as orphans; I will come to you. Before long, the world will not see me anymore, but you will see me.*
> *Because I live, you also will live. On that day you will realize that I am in my Father, and you are in me, and I am in you.*
>
> John 14:18-20

He will not leave us as orphans. He and His Father will come and live in us!

> *Jesus replied, "If anyone loves me, he will obey my teaching. My Father will love him, and we will come to him and make our home with him."*
>
> John 14:23

This is a new relationship, one that is completely unknown to the Jewish people. God has APPEARED TO THEM, as He did to Moses in the burning bush and to the children of Israel in the wilderness in a cloud of fire. He has now LIVED AMONG THEM in the person of His Son, the Lord Jesus Christ.

But now all three persons of the Godhead are going TO LIVE IN THEM. The disciples are going to be continually in His presence!

As born-again believers, are we experiencing that truth in our own lives? Are we continually in His presence?

Jesus came to give us life, not religion! Religion is something that we do. Relationship is something that God does in and for us.

Not only does the Father want us to know we have a home in Him, but He also wants to build His home in us. He wants a resting place.

> *This is what the LORD says: "Heaven is my throne and the earth is my footstool. Where is the house you will build for me? Where will my resting place be?"*
>
> Isaiah 66:1

When Father establishes His home in us, then we have a place we can go where He is always present. Never alone, we can feel safe and secure, knowing we are loved and accepted, sensing His delight in us.

> *The LORD your God is with you, he is mighty to save. He will take great delight in you, he will quiet you with his love, he will rejoice over you with singing.*
>
> Zephaniah 3:17

What makes a house a home?

It's not the type of building or the number of people who live in it. A small apartment in an inner-city ghetto can be home, while a large mansion overlooking a 400-acre country estate can be a "living arrangement."

Love. Intimacy. Relationship. It's what happens inside those four walls among the people who share the space that ultimately makes the difference.

The older son lives in his father's house, but he doesn't know his father's heart. He doesn't know what his father expects of him. He doesn't even know what is his.

The Old Testament Law has become this older son's taskmaster. Driven to achieve, he is caught on a merciless treadmill that allows him no way to get off.

How can this older son take off his sandals, relax, and just be himself when he has to spend his days in the field, working hard to please his father and earn a place in his heart?

Yes, he's living in his father's house. But he doesn't know what it means to be at home!

The father, knowing this and grieving for his son, says:

"My son," the father said, "you are always with me, and every-thing I have is yours."

Luke 15:31

If only his older son could grasp this truth, what he wants and so desperately needs would be his!

His older son would stop striving. He would relax. He would be himself.

Gone would be the fear of failure, rejection, and abandonment. Why? *"You are always with me"* (v. 31) says the father.

Is this a mere statement of fact? No. It is a call to freedom. No matter where his son goes, no matter what he does, he can know that his father's presence goes with him!

As a father he is giving his son permission to fail, to make mistakes, and to find his own way. Performance is no longer an issue. A loving, caring relationship is at stake.

For he knows that intimacy demands honesty and he wants to share EVERYTHING with his older son, even his son's most painful experiences of failure and personal rejection. So, as a father, he is reassuring him by using the word *always*. He is telling him that his love for him is unconditional.

There is no fear in love. But perfect love drives out fear,
because fear has to do with punishment. The one who fears is
not made perfect in love.

1 John 4:18

This is a picture of our Heavenly Father. He wants to share EVERYTHING with us as His children, even our most painful experiences of failure and personal rejection.

Many of us, like the older son, are legalistic and insecure. We want to relate to God on the basis of performance. But when we come to know the Father as He knows Himself to be, we can experience the unconditional love and acceptance He has for us in Christ.

When Jesus Christ died for our sins—past, present, and future—what separated us from an intimate, loving relationship with our Heavenly Father (the Law) was dealt with on the cross, once for all. Now the law of the Spirit (grace) sets us free.

> *Therefore, there is now no condemnation for those who are in*
> *Christ Jesus, because through Christ Jesus the law of the Spirit*
> *of life set me free from the law of sin and death.*
>
> Romans 8:1-2

We can stop striving. We can relax. We can be ourselves. We don't have to be afraid of failure, rejection, or even abandonment.

Father is ALWAYS with us!

So how do we come to experience this truth as a reality in our own lives?

We acknowledge the Father's presence. We talk to Him. We include Him in our activities. We believe and we act, knowing He is there.[6]

For example, when we are going to the grocery store, we realize that He is with us. We tell Him how our day went, and we discuss our plans for tomorrow.

When we remember a painful experience from our childhood, we share it with the Him, asking Him as our Heavenly Father to give us the parenting and support we needed but did not receive in the past.

When we are considering a change in employment, we share our plans and concerns, asking Him for His counsel and direction.

Most of us believe that Father is with us when we attend church services or when we pray. Do we also believe that He is with us when we go to the beach to swim or to the department store to buy a pair of shoes?

Isn't that what the word *always* means? No matter where we go, no matter what we do, His presence goes with us.

A house is a place. A home is a relationship.

When we begin to grasp the truth in the words. *"You are always with me"* (v. 31), we can begin to experience an intimate relationship with the Father that will meet our deepest need for love.

We can be at home with God. We can kick off our shoes, relax, and just be ourselves. We can even make mistakes.

From Elder Son to Prodigal

"In Jesus' parable of The Prodigal Son," said Bill, "the elder brother is the good boy who never quite makes it as a son in his father's house. I've spent most of my life being that good boy who was never really sure he had a place in his father's heart.

"For whatever reason, I felt I was in competition with my younger brother, who was as secure as I was insecure. Although I had some gifts in greater proportion to those that he had, for the most part I discounted them.

"I worked hard to win my father's approval and I suspect, looking back, that he did affirm me. The sad truth is that I never really trusted in his love or his favor.

"Many of the things I did do that were good, I did to build myself up in the eyes of others, not for the love of doing them, or for the love of God. Performance orientation was my idol and it kept me hopelessly in bondage.

"I carried all of this emotional baggage into my marriage and ministry, doing great damage to both. The need to prove myself and my own self-worth was never really satiated.

"Later, as I was exposed to the church-growth literature, my reading fanned the lusty flame that burned within me. I wanted to be a successful pastor and I knew that meant numbers.

"So I began to coax my board and church into applying some of the ideas that had proven effective in other churches. God was opening the way for us, or so I thought. Yet resistance, mostly passive, rewarded my efforts.

"I pulled away from those who were unwilling to support me as the numbers in attendance on Sunday morning instead of increasing, suddenly began to dwindle.

"Struggling with what seemingly had become a joyless ministry, I ceased to be much of a pastor. Deeply discouraged, I felt that God was making my life unbearable, asking me to do what He had never equipped me to do.

"Little did I realize that the enemy of my soul was right there, watching, waiting, setting a trap to bring me down. But when the bait was presented by a woman in the church who wanted me as a lover, I eagerly took it.

"The affair was pure rebellion—a self-pitying, self-destructive act of defiance against God, myself, my wife, my friends, and my church. But in the midst of failure I was determined to have some pleasure along with my pain.

"Then with public confession came my resignation as pastor. Suddenly life was over. Shameful failure was now the sum total of a lifetime of effort. I had no claim to anyone's acceptance, much less their approval.

"As an elder brother I had become the prodigal in the far country. Now I could literally die or go home a washed-up fool. I went home.

"My wife, of course, was terribly hurt. I could not have imagined the depth of her pain. But what was even more astounding was that she continued to love me in spite of it.

"As my own pastor, his wife, and some friends came alongside with Father's healing love, instead of the condemnation I so richly deserved, they, too, became revealers of God's amazing grace, extended by the Lord Jesus to a sinner who had nothing but his sin to offer in return.

"Could I have received this healing love before my fall? Probably not! I had to be broken before Him.

"Now by grace 'Our Father' has become 'My Father.' I know Father loves me and has always loved me. He has never turned His back on me, even when I was deep in sin.

"Father has brought me to full repentance, and in Jesus' atonement has freely given me everything I've spent a lifetime trying to earn. It is to this God I so willingly and gladly surrender.

"Now the only life I have is Jesus' life—to go where He wants me to go, to do what He wants me to do. It is really true, not a boast, that all I am, all I have now belongs to Him.

"As His purpose for my life unfolds, I find myself drawn to those in jails and prisons who, like me, have made a mess of their lives and know it. It is to these people that I go, eagerly, to share the Gospel for which I live and have so recently discovered, 'It is the power of God unto salvation for everyone who believes.'

"Once an elder son, then a prodigal, now I, too, by His glorious grace am a son of the Heavenly Father!"

Looking for
a Daddy to Love

"Jack, when I was four years old my mother and father were divorced. Even back that far, I can remember wanting to relate to a father," said Robert.

"First I looked at my Sunday school teacher and wondered what kind of daddy he would be. Then when I began school I would look at the principal and the superintendent and wonder what kind of daddy each of them would be.

"Everywhere I went I was looking for a father image.

"When I reached puberty, I started getting other thoughts—perverted thoughts that really troubled me. I hated these thoughts, but I didn't know how to get rid of them.

"I went to college, heard about Jesus, and accepted Him as my Savior. Surely, I thought, my conversion will break the power of these thoughts. But it didn't.

"I decided to go into the ministry, but even becoming a pastor did not stop the thoughts from troubling me.

"Then I got married to prove to myself and to others that I wasn't 'that kind of man.' But even though I could function in a marriage relationship as a heterosexual, the thoughts continued to torment me.

"Finally, I went to a pastoral counseling clinic and was told that a good way to get victory over a problem like this is to find a trusted man in your congregation and confide in him. They quoted the Scripture:

Therefore confess your sins to each other and pray for each other so that you may be healed.

James 5:16a

"So I went back home and shared my struggle with a man in the church whom I trusted. But this man, who couldn't handle my confession, told his friend, who told his friend. The next thing I knew, it was all over town that 'Pastor is a homosexual.'

"There was absolutely nothing I could do about the accusation. So I resigned from the church and left the ministry."

[Robert had never been involved in a homosexual act.]

So I said, "Brother, I believe you have a deep emotional need that you have perceived as a moral problem. Do you think you could become that little boy who has lost his daddy and who needs to be loved?"

"I'll sure try," he said.

So I took Robert in my arms, and as I began to pray, he wept.

"Robert, you weren't only hurt because you did not have a father to love you. You were hurt because you didn't have a daddy to love. I'd like you to be that little boy now and hug me as a son would hug his daddy."

When Robert hugged me, he wept some more. Then he pushed himself back and said, "Jack, you won't believe what has just happened to me. I have never been able to hug a man. Now the fear, the perverted thoughts are gone!"

Some months passed. Then one night, as I was about to begin a week-long seminar on *The Father Heart of God*, a man walked up, smiled, and threw his arms around me.

"Remember me?"

"I sure do!" I said.

Yes, you guessed it. That man was Robert. The love of the Father had set him free!

*Can we say to Him from the depths
of our heart, without hesitation: "You are always
with me, and everything I have is Yours"?
Or are there some areas of our lives
that are "off limits," even to God?*

Chapter Eleven

The Inheritance

"My son," the father said, "you are always with me, and everything I have is yours."

Luke 15:31

If we never ask or let people know what we need, we can end up like Bill, Robert, or the older son: frustrated, empty-handed, and very, very angry.

It's only when we humble ourselves and ask, that we can receive and experience the joy of having our needs met.

Ask. Receive. Ask. Receive.

Now that's a basic principle that even a small child can understand. Take him to a grocery store and he will have no inhibitions about asking for a bag of candy that is hanging on a peg in front of the checkout lane. Ignore his request and he will reach for the bag on his own.

Even a newborn baby will cry until someone comes and changes his wet diaper, fills his tummy with a warm bottle of milk, or holds him close. He knows from firsthand experience that persistence is the key. If no one responds, he simply continues his cries and increases the volume!

Then why is it that we as adults have such a hard time getting our own needs met?

- "It's selfish to ask. It's putting myself first when I should be thinking of others."
- "I'm afraid. If I ask, they might say 'no' and I would be disappointed."
- "I feel ashamed. I don't want others to know I have a need."

- "If they help me, I'll have to help them in return, and I can't do that."
- "Adults don't have needs. They can take care of themselves."

Recognize any of these statements? They may sound like good reasons for not sharing our needs with others and with the Father. But when we take a closer look, we will see them for what they are: lies from the enemy.

Most of our excuses are a smoke screen for an even bigger problem: pride. It takes humility to ask.

Some of us, like this older son, may be so out of tune with what is going on inside of us, that we may not know what we need or even recognize that we have a need. Then the Word says we can come to the Father and He will give us wisdom.

> *If any of you lacks wisdom, he should ask God, who gives generously to all without finding fault, and it will be given to him.*
>
> James 1:5

Some of us may live under the false assumption that others will recognize our need and automatically meet it without our saying a word. That's a nice idea, but in real life it rarely works that way, does it?

This "mind reading" approach seems to run rampant, especially at Christmas time. Our husband (or wife) will ask us for a list of gift ideas and we respond by saying, "Oh, just surprise me, honey! You know what I want."

Then, when Christmas morning arrives and there under the tree is the wrong size box for what we were hoping to receive, we realize that a brown tie with small dots is not a pair of golf clubs, and a three-speed blender is not a pair of diamond earrings!

We are disappointed—again. Why? We didn't ask for what we really wanted!

That's why the older son in Luke's parable did not receive his party. As far as we know, he never told his father that he wanted one!

Some of us assume that because our Heavenly Father is omniscient (all-knowing), He will automatically meet our needs without our asking Him to do so. Now it is certainly true that Father knows what we need.

*Do not be like them [the pagans], for your Father knows what
you need before you ask him.*

Matthew 6:8

But the Word of God says He still waits for us to ask!

*Until now you have not asked for anything in my name. Ask and
you will receive, and your joy will be complete.*

John 16:24

Why? So when we receive what we ask for, we will know it is from the
Father and our joy will be complete!

The second truth this father shares with his older son concerns inheritance and what is already his: *"...and everything I have is yours"* (v. 31).

Love, an intimate relationship, even a joyous celebration! It has already
been provided. All he has to do is reach out, take what is his, and receive it
as a gift.

Now my children have always been free to help themselves to anything that is in our refrigerator. But if one of them were to come to me and
say, "Dad, I'm hungry. Can I make myself a cheese sandwich?" I'd say
"yes" and not give the question a second thought.

However, if that same child of mine were to come back time and time
again, asking my permission to take something from our refrigerator, I
would be concerned.

If my children believe what I have said, the matter is settled. They
will help themselves to whatever is in our refrigerator. If they don't
believe what I have said, they will never feel free to take what is already
theirs.

That's the truth that this father is trying to share with his older son.
Anything his son needs or wants is already his—even a young goat for a
celebration.

The property has already been divided. In fact, as the oldest son, he
has received twice as much as his younger brother—a double portion!

He doesn't have to work hard to earn it. He doesn't have to be on his
best behavior to deserve it. All he has to do is believe what his father has
said and claim what is his!

The same is true of our Heavenly Father. He owns the cattle on a thousand hills.

For every animal of the forest is mine, and the cattle on a thousand hills.

Psalm 50:10

As children of God, we are co-heirs with Christ. Everything our Father has is ours! All we have to do is claim it!

The Spirit himself testifies with our spirit that we are God's children. Now if we are children, then we are heirs— heirs of God and co-heirs with Christ, if indeed we share in his sufferings in order that we may also share in his glory.

Romans 8:16-17

Finally, a loving, intimate relationship involves more than one person. For us to be at home with the Father, He also must be at home with us.

Now my wife, Dorothy, and I have been married for over 40 years. We have a loving, intimate relationship that is based on mutual trust. We respect each other.

If either of us had a financial need, the other would share whatever he or she had to meet that need. If I were away from the house, Dorothy would feel free to take whatever she needed from my billfold. If she were away from the house, I'd feel free to go to her purse.

That's the kind of relationship we have. Everything I have is hers. Everything she has is mine. We trust each other with our possessions, with our very lives.

An intimate, loving relationship is based on mutual trust. Is that the kind of relationship we have with our Heavenly Father?

Do we trust Him with our possessions, with our very lives?

Can we give Him free access to our money, our time, our car, our friendships, our choice of a marriage partner or place of employment?

Can we say to Him from the depths of our heart, without hesitation: "You are always with me, and everything I have is Yours"? Or are there some areas of our lives that are "off limits," even to God?

When we know the love of the Father and His heart for us, we have confidence. We know we can rely on His love.

And so we know and rely on the love God has for us. God is love. Whoever lives in love lives in God, and God in him.

1 John 4:16

This allows us to give our hearts—and yes, even our very lives—to Him. Why? Our love for Him compels us.

The older son does not know his father's heart. So all he can do is serve his father out of obligation and relate to him as a servant would to a master. He has little to look forward to—only what he can earn.

While the younger son, who is beginning to know his father's heart, can serve his father out of gratitude. Love compels him.

Everything is a big word, even to the more mature in Christ among us. But that's because, like the older son, we've settled for religion and bypassed relationship.

We need to ask ourselves, "Whom am I serving, and why?"

If I speak in the tongues of men and of angels, but have not love, I am only a resounding gong or a clanging cymbal. If I have the gift of prophecy and can fathom all mysteries and all knowledge, and if I have a faith that can move mountains. but have not love, I am nothing. If I give all I possess to the poor and surrender my body to the flames, but have not love, I gain nothing.

1 Corinthians 13:1-3

Even if we give everything we have to the poor and allow ourselves to be martyred for the cause of Christ, if we have not love, we gain nothing. Nothing.

This is the older son's dilemma. He has everything given to him, but at the same time he has nothing. Why? Without love, his life is empty, meaningless.

So how do we receive the love we need?

We love because he first loved us.

1 John 4:19

We allow the Father to love us FIRST. Then out of that love relationship flows love for ourselves and for others.

Have we experienced the Father's love? Have we given ourselves to Him so He can touch the very depths of our being?

He will. All we have to do is ask.

Everything He has—including His fathomless love—is ours!

"It's Your Birthday!"

"For some time I had felt there was something missing in my relationship with the Father," said Linda, "some barrier to truly knowing Him and receiving His love.

"With anticipation and expectancy I had prayed, 'Lord, I want to know You. Just as my friend, Diana, has met You, I want to meet You, too.'

"As I waited on the Lord, I could hear the Spirit say, 'Jesus is coming. Do you hear Him, Linda?'

"At first I didn't hear anything. But then, as the sound of the music came nearer, I answered, 'Yes, Lord, I hear Him. Is it a parade?'

"'No,' the Lord replied, 'it's a party, your party. It's your birthday—a celebration of the day you were born!'

"This had great significance for me for several reasons. First, I had a fear of parties—of participating and of being left out.

"Second, I'd had only one party as a child and it had been a total disaster. Mother had prepared snacks. Then she had sent us out to the camper, leaving the entertainment up to me.

"The pressure of that evening was such that I could not enjoy any part of it. I felt abandoned.

"Third, the Lord had said it was my 'birth' day. A number of years before, God had revealed to me that I had not wanted to be born.

"So the idea of a party brought a mixed response of 'Wow' and 'Oh, no' at the same time. Fear rose up in me as I watched the party approach.

"The party was still a long distance away and it didn't seem to be coming any closer. So I wondered what was wrong.

"'What do I need to do to get to the party?' I asked myself. The Lord gave me the answer from the Gospel of John:

Father, I want those you have given me to be with me where I am, and to see my glory, the glory you have given me because you loved me before the creation of the world.

John 17:24

"'Jesus,' I prayed, 'the Word says that this party is for me. You want to be with me and I want to be with You. You want me to see Your glory. What is Your glory?'

"'My glory is My relationship with My Father. He loved Me before the creation of the world. He also loved you and chose you in Me before the creation of the world. You have always been loved!'

"'So how do I get to the party? What do I have to do?'

"'Receive Me.'

"'Receive You, Jesus? That's it?'

"'That's it! The party is coming to you, Linda!'

"'Jesus,' I said, 'I receive You. You are life. You are the party.'

"I felt the Spirit of God come on me and His presence inside of me. Then I felt the party come in with Him.

"But I knew there was more. I wanted to meet the Father. I wanted to receive His love just like my friend, Diana, had when she prayed.

"'Lord,' I said, 'if it was that simple to receive a party, then it must be that simple to receive Your love. Your Word says that Your love is for me, so I receive Your love, Father.'

"As I waited expectantly on God, I suddenly saw myself as a little girl—three or four years old—skipping, dancing, asking Jesus a multitude of 'little girl' questions.

"'Where are we going?' I asked.

"'We're going to see the Father.'

"'Where is He? Is He hiding?'

"'No, He's running to meet you.'

"'Does He run fast?'

"Jesus laughed with delight.

"'Does the Father like little girls?'

"'Yes, He likes little girls,' He said.

"'Where is He now—still running?'

"'No, He's very close.'

"Fear rose up within me. Then Jesus looked directly into my eyes and said, 'It's okay. Don't be afraid.'

"'Okay,' I said. 'I will not be afraid. I will not fear.' Then I began to dance again.

"A wolf appeared in the path and I was afraid. Jesus said, 'Don't be afraid. I am your Shepherd.' He killed the wolf and we walked on.

"'Jesus, what does the Father look like?' I asked.

"'When you've seen Me, you've seen the Father.'

"'What's the Father like?'

"Jesus replied, 'He's just like Me. Am I kind?'

"'Yes, Jesus, You're kind.'

"Jesus replied, 'The Father is kind. Am I gentle?'

"'Yes, Jesus, You're gentle.'

"'The Father is gentle.'

"Then I sensed that the Father was there, close by, but I couldn't see Him. 'Jesus, why can't I see the Father? Is He hiding from me?'

"'No, Linda, He's waiting for you to invite Him to come closer.'

"Fear rose up within me, and immediately Jesus was beside me. I said, 'I will not fear,' and with a trembling voice I said, 'It's okay, Father. You can come closer.'

"Again fear rose up within me. Jesus was right there. I said, 'I will not fear. Come closer, Father.'

"Then I could see Him! I could see myself as that little girl, in His arms, and He was loving me.

"I watched for a while, but the scene seemed somehow removed. I wanted to know it was *my heart*. So I invited Him to come closer.

"'Come closer, Father,' I repeated, as the Father came closer. Soon it became, 'Come closer, Daddy.'

"The presence of God became so strong that I felt some kind of transformation take place deep within. I looked like I had become a little baby, perhaps two months old, snuggled up against the Father's neck. He was loving on me, stroking my back, kissing my face.

"He smiled and said, 'You did it!'

"'I did what?' I asked.

"'You accepted your birth. You are a gift from Me!'

"In the background I could hear cheering. Still I wanted more. 'Daddy, hold me closer. Hold me tight.'

"The presence of God was so strong, so heavy, I could barely move, barely breathe. 'I receive Your love, Daddy. Bathe me in it.'

"Wave upon wave of pure love washed over me and through me. I drank it in, reveled in it. I could feel God's kisses.

"'Daddy,' I said, 'if we are really this close, I should be able to feel Your heartbeat against my body. Let me feel Your heartbeat in my body.'

"And He did. It felt like my heart was double-beating—first my heartbeat, then His heartbeat.

"This experience lasted for almost an hour. At one point the Father told me that I would never be the same. How true!

"I now know God's love for me. I know what it is like to joyfully put my arms around His neck and call Him 'Abba, Daddy.'

"Where before there was reserve, formality, even an aversion to calling Him 'Dad,' now there is closeness without fear. His perfect, pure love has cast out the fear."

"Will He Have a
Party for Me, Too?"

Andrew said he had really blown it. He had sinned against God, his wife, his children, and the body of Christ.

"What have you done?" I asked.

"Just terrible things," he said. "I am so ashamed, so mad at myself I just can't believe it."

"What have you done?" I asked.

"My wife caught me exposing myself, a problem I've had for more than 25 years. When she left I said, 'To hell with Christianity. To hell with Christ. It doesn't work.'

"Since then I've been drunk every night and I've been going to strip joints. I'm just really in a mess.

"One night I knew my parents were gone and I knew where the key to the house was hidden. So I went and stole $3,000. I spent $500 of it on the strippers, asking them to dance for me. I also solicited the services of a prostitute."

"Have you come to the end of yourself? Are you willing to repent?"

"I don't know," Andrew said, "if I even know how to repent."

"Father's arms are open wide. In fact, He is running to meet you. Are you willing to let Him love you?"

"HOW CAN HE LOVE ME?" Andrew said. "I can't even love myself."

"This is the love of God," I said, "unconditional love that is based on the righteousness of Christ. You're in the pigpen, but you're a sheep—not a pig. Father wants to take you out of that mud and take you into His arms."

"BUT HOW CAN HE LOVE ME?"

"Love is His nature," I said, "but you'll have to humble yourself, Andrew, to receive it. You'll have to allow Him to love you."

As I held Andrew in my arms, he wept and Father's healing love began to penetrate his empty heart. Then I said, "Are you willing to forgive yourself?"

"How can I? No, I won't," he said. "I can't forgive myself for all the things I've done."

"If God can forgive you," I said, "if God is willing to accept you, you need to accept and forgive yourself. You need to stop playing God. Are you more righteous than He is?"

Andrew wept and wept. Then as he humbled himself and forgave himself for all that he had done, Father began to restore him.

Finally I said, "Now Father wants to clothe you with a festal robe, put a ring on your finger and sandals on your feet."

By this time Andrew was laughing. "Will He have a party for me, too?"

If our sin has been public, so should our forgiveness and restoration be made public. There should be a celebration—an end to the shame.

Chapter Twelve

The Celebration

*But we had to celebrate and be glad, because this brother
of yours was dead and is alive again; he was lost and is found.*

Luke 15:32

We had to celebrate" (v. 32) says the father to his older son.
Why? When a sinner comes home, there is always a cele-
bration. That's the way the Father responds to our repentance. He rejoices!
He throws a party!

*In the same way, I tell you, there is rejoicing in the presence of
the angels of God over one sinner who repents.*

Luke 15:10

How many of us are like this older son? How many of us out of anger
or disgust would have refused to go to the party and stayed at home?

After all, this is a prodigal who has hit bottom. This is a Jewish son
who has wasted his inheritance, slept with prostitutes, been involved in
riotous living, and fed swine for a living.

Let's be honest. How many of us would want to be seen with this type
of individual, let alone celebrate his return?

This is the problem that Jesus is having with the scribes and
Pharisees. Even as He speaks, the tax collectors and "sinners" are gather-
ing around to hear what He has to say.

*But the Pharisees and the teachers of the law muttered, "This
man welcomes sinners and eats with them."*

Luke 15:2

Tongues are wagging. What is wrong with this Jesus of Nazareth that He would lower Himself to rub elbows with the "sinners" among them?

How about us? As brothers and sisters in Christ are we, like Jesus, willing to welcome and even eat with the "sinners" among us? Are we willing to celebrate as the prodigals come home?

Or, like the lesser parent, are we keeping our distance? Are we outlining conditions for their return?

Are we waiting for them to crawl to the altar on their hands and knees, weep, and give a long public confession? Are we receiving them on a "probationary status"—letting months, perhaps even years pass by as we watch them from a distance to see if their repentance is truly sincere?

Or are we standing at the door with our Heavenly Father, waiting and interceding for the prodigals' return? Are we running to meet them, throwing our arms around them, and even giving them our best robe? Are we loving them as the Father loves us—unconditionally?

Perhaps it's a matter of priority. In the parable of the great banquet, we see three guests who are too involved in their own affairs to come.

> *When one of those at the table with him heard this, he said to Jesus, "Blessed is the man who will eat at the feast in the kingdom of God." Jesus replied: "A certain man was preparing a great banquet and invited many guests. At the time of the banquet he sent his servant to tell those who had been invited, 'Come, for everything is now ready.' But they all alike began to make excuses."*

Luke 14:15-18a

As was the custom in the East, a double invitation had been extended. The first invitation was given sometime before the banquet was to be served. Then, when the time drew near, a servant had been sent out a second time to announce that everything was ready!

So these guests have had plenty of advance warning. But when the servant arrives the second time, *"they all alike began to make excuses"* (v. 18).

One guest has just bought a field and has to go and see it (v. 18). A second guest has purchased five yoke of oxen and needs to go and prove them (v. 19). A third guest has just gotten married (v. 20).

What is the response of the owner of the house? Anger.

Then the owner of the house became angry and ordered his servant, "Go out quickly into the streets and alleys of the town and bring in the poor, the crippled, the blind and the lame."

Luke 14:21b

No one who throws a party wants his invitation to be turned down, especially when the excuse is so flimsy. The first guest should have gone to see the field before he bought it; the second guest should have tried out the five yoke of oxen before he purchased them; and the third guest should have brought his wife!

We all have excuses or reasons why we can't celebrate. Some are more valid or believable than others.

If we are performance-oriented, we may see parties as frivolous or a waste of time. Fun may be an afterthought—like the saying goes: Work now, play later.

If we don't know how to party, it may be a matter of pride or personal discomfort.

In the Father's eyes and in the economy of heaven, celebration is a top priority. If we don't see the return of a prodigal as reason to drop whatever we are doing and party, we need to seek His forgiveness. The heart of the Father, like the heart of the father in the parable, is to go after that one which is lost and rejoice when he is found!

But in the case of this older son, his refusal to join the celebration is not a matter of priority or of personal discomfort. It is a response born in deep-seated anger.

In self-righteous indignation he is saying, "I will not celebrate the return of a sinner, even if he is my own brother! He deserves death, not a party!"

Then the parable of the great banquet goes on to say:

"Sir," the servant said, "what you ordered has been done, but there is still room." Then the master told his servant, "Go out to the roads and country lanes and make them come in, so that my house will be full."

Luke 14:22-23

In essence, what this owner is saying to his servant is: "Invite the misfits! Compel them to come in!"

To "compel" a guest to come is a custom unknown in the Western world, where we are used to a brief invitation and an almost immediate reply. But in the East this type of brief invitation would be seen as very undignified.

A guest, although he would plan to attend, would be expected to refuse the first invitation, so the host would have the privilege of "compelling him" to accept on the second invitation.

Jesus came to die for the sins of the world, for all of us. But when He was here on earth, His ministry was to the Jews, the chosen of God. It was only later, after Pentecost, that His disciples would begin to take the good news of the Gospel to the Gentiles.

This is what is happening here. The first invitation is going out to those who, by the standards of the religious leaders of the day, are most deserving of such an honor. But once that invitation is refused, it is again being extended to anyone who will respond—even the misfits!

The last verse is probably the saddest declaration of all.

> *I tell you, not one of those men who were invited will get a taste of my banquet.*
>
> Luke 14:24

For all of us there comes that day when the door of opportunity is closed and the invitation is withdrawn.

> *The Lord is not slow in keeping his promise, as some understand slowness. He is patient with you, not wanting anyone to perish, but everyone to come to repentance. But the day of the Lord will come like a thief. The heavens will disappear with a roar; the elements will be destroyed by fire, and the earth and everything in it will be laid bare.*
>
> 2 Peter 3:9-10

We may want to join the party on our own terms in our own time, but when the door is closed, we will be turned away.

For whom does the father throw a party? The prodigal—the son who has sinned.

For whom is there *"rejoicing in the presence of the angels of God"*? For the *"sinner who repents"* (Luke 15:10).

That's why the older son cannot join the party. In his own eyes, he is not a sinner.

> *But the LORD said to Samuel, "Do not consider his appearance*
> *or his height, for I have rejected him. The LORD does not look at*
> *the things man looks at. Man looks at the outward appearance,*
> *but the LORD looks at the heart."*
>
> 1 Samuel 16:7

The older son is judging himself by what he sees on the outside—his behavior, while God is judging him by what He sees on the inside—the older son's heart.

Also, like many of us, this older son is ranking sin by degree, i.e. seeing disobedience as more reprehensible than pride, and a rebellious spirit as more deserving of punishment than an unforgiving heart. But in God's eyes, there is no distinction. Sin is sin.

It is only when we see ourselves as the Father sees us, sinners saved by grace, that we can join the party and welcome the prodigals home. For then we are able to remember when we, too, deserved death, but instead received a joyous homecoming!

Father loves parties! One of His greatest celebrations occurred on the day of Pentecost!

For 40 days Jesus had walked among them, giving *"many convincing proofs that he was alive"* (Acts 1:3a).

> *On one occasion, while he was eating with them, he gave them*
> *this command: "Do not leave Jerusalem, but wait for the gift*
> *my Father promised, which you have heard me speak about. For*
> *John baptized with water, but in a few days you will be baptized*
> *with the Holy Spirit."*
>
> Acts 1:4-5

Then every demon stood by in amazement as Father gave the world its first glimpse of "the church of grace"—120 men and women, drunk not on wine, but on the Holy Spirit! What a party!

As far as we know, the older son never joins the celebration. Perhaps this is also true of the scribes and the Pharisees who, as Jesus tells the parable, go away, never accepting or identifying with the tax collectors and the "sinners" in their midst.

Are we like this older son? Have we received an invitation to join the celebration and refused to go in?

Let's not miss the party! Let's dance before the throne of God and welcome the prodigals home!

If our sin has been public, so should our forgiveness and restoration be made public. There should be a celebration—an end to the shame.

Part IV:
❧ The Third Son ☙

A Father's Embrace

Hyung Ho picked me up at the airport. "I have two daughters," he said.

"The younger one, Kyung Hee, is in her freshman year at university and is doing very well in her studies. As a family we are all very proud of her. The older one, Soon Hee, is still living at home and helps us in the store."

I knew this dad loved both of his daughters, but I couldn't help but sense some disappointment in his voice as he talked about Soon Hee.

After the seminar Hyung Ho came to me and said: "Jack, I never realized until I heard you speak this morning how much I had missed as a child, growing up in a home where I did not know the love of a father. I guess you could say I was a survivor. My own father died in the Korean War shortly after I was born.

"This afternoon as we prayed, I wept. The pain in my heart was so deep. I don't think I have ever cried like that in my entire life.

"As you were holding me in your arms, like a father would hold his small son, I realized how good it felt to be embraced. For so long my heart has been empty, crying out for a kind of love that neither my wife nor my daughters could ever give.

"Jack, I still need a dad. How wonderful it is to know that God is my Father! As His child I can rest secure in the knowledge that He loves and cares for me, with no strings attached.

"I'm not the same man who picked you up at the airport. I'm different, changed in a way that is hard for me to put into words.

"Now I want to go home and be a father to my own daughters. Never having known the embrace of a loving father, I realize that I, too, have failed my family. I have never hugged my own children, even when they were very, very small."

When the seminar was over Hyung Ho went back to the city. Determined to keep his promise to the Lord, he immediately walked into the family store, took Soon Hee in his arms, and gave her the biggest bear hug a father could ever give a daughter.

Surprised, but pleased, Soon Hee wept, then smiled, right in front of the customers she had been waiting on!

"I didn't care," said Hyung Ho, "what people thought. It felt so good to love my daughter and be free enough to show it.

"Now my heart is overflowing with love for my family, my God, and for others. It is truly a miracle. For the first time in my life I know I am loved. I know that God is my Father!"

"Today You're Going to Meet My Dad!"

"I had been a Christian for ten years," said Carol, "and had come to know Jesus not only as Lord and Savior, but as Friend and Beloved. Still, something was missing in my spiritual life.

"One day while I was serving on the staff at Youth With A Mission, I experienced an emotional breakdown. I felt clearly directed by the Lord to seek help from the mission's counseling clinic and began six weeks of intensive spiritual and emotional 'renewing.'

"During one session I was asked if I had ever met the Father. I thought, 'I know Jesus and I know the Holy Spirit, but do I know the Father?'

"My two counselors began praying over me, and a vision as colorful as life began playing before my eyes. This is what I saw.

"Jesus was standing next to a little girl about three or four years of age (I knew immediately that I was that little girl) and said, 'Today you're going to meet My Dad!'

"He took me by the hand and, after walking a short distance, we saw a man standing in wait. He appeared taller than Jesus, yet not really. He seemed older than Jesus, yet young.

"His hair was a magnificent, shoulder-length mass of white. I looked up at Him and said, 'Gee! You sure have bushy hair!' His obvious delight was apparent in the hearty way He threw back His head and laughed.

"Then He said, 'Carol, would you like to sit on My lap?' I answered by gingerly climbing onto His knees. Immediately a sense of safety, love, and acceptance filled my being.

"Confidently, I placed my arm around His neck and pressed my head against His chest. I could hear His heart beating. Contentment began to flood through my body in giant waves.

"Suddenly I looked down and to my amazement I was wearing a beautiful white party dress, white lace-trimmed socks, and shiny black patent leather shoes. I had never felt so pampered or so special in my entire life!

"The scene ended and I was back in the counseling room, remembering a question I had asked the Lord several weeks earlier: 'Who am I really, Lord?'

"He had answered, 'Why, Carol, you're My little girl!' I didn't understand His answer then, but I do now.

"I don't have to be an 'adult' with my Heavenly Father or perform to be pleasing in His sight. I don't have to do anything but BE—a little girl always needing her Dad and always knowing she is loved and wanted by Him.

"This happened nine years ago and since then the Father has continued to reveal Himself to me in many ways. He is changing and healing me for His own pleasure. And mine.

"My heart is so full of gratitude to my Father who loves me with a never-ending, unconditional love. He is teaching me how to love Him in return and how to minister His love to others."

The goal and climax of New Testament revelation is the Father. If we stop with knowing Jesus, or experiencing the power of the Holy Spirit, then we will stop short of the revelation and the relationship that Jesus died to give us.

Chapter Thirteen

Knowing Him

Now there's a third son that we need to look at—the Son who is telling the story. Jesus also left His Father's house (heaven's glory) to go to a far country (planet earth):

> *But we see Jesus, who was made a little lower than the angels, now crowned with glory and honor because he suffered death, so that by the grace of God he might taste death for everyone.*
>
> Hebrews 2:9

associated with harlots, drunkards, tax collectors, and "sinners":

> *Now the tax collectors and "sinners" were all gathering around to hear him. But the Pharisees and the teachers of the law muttered, "This man welcomes sinners and eats with them."*
>
> Luke 15:1-2

was tempted in all points as we are:

> *For we do not have a high priest who is unable to sympathize with our weaknesses, but we have one [Jesus] who has been tempted in every way, just as we are—yet was without sin.*
>
> Hebrews 4:15

and yet was without sin.

He became Immanuel (meaning "God with us") and so completely identified with our humanity that He was able to destroy the powers of evil:

> *Since the children have flesh and blood, he too shared in their*
> *humanity so that by his death he might destroy him who holds*
> *the power of death—that is, the devil—and free those who all*
> *their lives were held in slavery by their fear of death.*
>
> Hebrews 2:14-15

reconcile us through His death on the cross, and bring us to the Father.

> *For God was pleased to have all his fullness dwell in him, and*
> *through him to reconcile to himself all things, whether things*
> *on earth or things in heaven, by making peace through his*
> *blood, shed on the cross.*
>
> Colossians 1:19-20

The reason Jesus can tell this story and reveal the love of the Father is because He and the Father are one!

> *I and the Father are one.*
>
> John 10:30

He is in intimate relationship with the Father and always has been, as shown in the Gospel of John, where He is referred to as the Word.

> *In the beginning was the Word, and the Word was with God,*
> *and the Word was God. He was with God in the beginning.*
> *Through him all things were made; without him nothing was*
> *made that has been made. In him was life, and that life was the*
> *light of men.*
>
> John 1:1-4

Jesus was in the very beginning, when all things were created.

As the Son of God, Jesus is in total submission to His Father. The works He does are not His works. The words He speaks are not His words. They are the works and the words of His Father who is *"living in"* Him.

Don't you believe that I am in the Father, and that the Father is in me? The words I say to you are not just my own. Rather, it is the Father, living in me, who is doing his work.

John 14:10

In fact, Jesus' mission or primary goal in terms of public ministry is to reveal the Father and His limitless love for the sinner to the world.

If you really knew me, you would know my Father as well. From now on, you do know him and have seen him.

John 14:7

For God so loved the world that he gave his one and only Son, that whoever believes in him shall not perish but have eternal life.

John 3:16

When Philip, one of the disciples, asks Jesus to show him the Father, Jesus replies:

Don't you know me, Philip, even after I have been among you such a long time? Anyone who has seen me has seen the Father. How can you say, "Show us the Father"?

John 14:9

for Jesus is the exact representation of His Father's being, nature, and character.

The Son is the radiance of God's glory and the exact representation of his being, sustaining all things by his powerful word.

Hebrews 1:3a

The intimate relationship, the bonding that exists between the Son and the Father is so strong, so close that we cannot tell them apart. When we look at Jesus, we see the Father!

Can we fully grasp this truth from Scripture? Then let's stop, go back through the Gospels, and ask ourselves: Who took the children on His lap, prayed for them, and blessed them? Who drove the money changers from the temple? Who showed mercy to the woman caught in adultery? Who washed the disciples' feet in the Upper Room?

It was the Father, living in Jesus, who blessed the children, drove the money changers from the temple, showed mercy to the woman caught in adultery, and washed the disciples' feet!

When you have seen Me, says Jesus to Philip, you have seen the Father!

The goal and climax of New Testament revelation is the Father. If we stop with knowing Jesus or experiencing the power of the Holy Spirit, then we will stop short of the revelation and the relationship that Jesus died to give us.

Jesus came that we might have a personal relationship with the Father, that we might experience His love.

> *Jesus answered, "I am the way and the truth and the life. No one comes to the Father except through me."*
>
> John 14:6

When I became a Christian, John 14:6 was one of the first passages of Scripture that I memorized. I thought it was one of the most powerful proof texts concerning the deity of Christ.

I would tell people, "If you really want to know your sins are forgiven, Jesus is the Way! If you really want to know you have eternal life, Jesus is the Way!"

Both of these statements are true. But many years would pass before I would realize the spiritual truth behind this verse.

Jesus is saying, "I am the Way for you to experience the fathering you did not receive as a child. I am the Way for you to experience the unconditional love your heart is crying out for. Through My death on the cross, I am providing the Way TO THE FATHER!"

Many of us live defeated, messed-up lives because we have not received the right kind of parenting as children. Jesus wants to bring us out of that bondage into an intimate relationship with His own Father so that we can begin to receive the fathering we so desperately need.

Then the Father will do what no one else can do. His love will reach to the very depths of our being and personality. He will begin to change us from the inside out!

One day I was teaching a seminar on *The Father Heart of God*. Right in the middle of my lecture a woman cried out, "My mother didn't love me. My father didn't love me. My brother didn't love me. I've never been loved. I don't know what it is to be loved!"

She was sitting next to her husband, but her need for love was so great that even he couldn't meet it! In fact, I had to stop the class, go over to where she was sitting, and minister to her. She was that upset.

Whether we realize it or not, that's what most of us are looking for—love. How do we develop an intimate relationship with the Father?

> *I tell you the truth, anyone who will not receive the*
> *kingdom of God like a little child will never enter it.*
>
> Luke 18:17

We humble ourselves and become as a little child. We allow Him to father us.

> *I in them and you in me. May they be brought to complete unity*
> *to let the world know that you sent me and have loved them*
> *even as you have loved me.*
>
> John 17:23

"I in them and you in me" (v. 23). If Father lives in Jesus and Jesus lives in me, then Father lives in me! If Father lives in Jesus and Jesus lives in you, then FATHER LIVES IN YOU!

This is the secret of indwelling—to have the Father LIVING IN US. We can't get any closer than that in terms of intimacy!

Then, like Jesus, the works we do are not our own works. The words we speak are not our own words. They are the works and the words of the Father who is *"living in"* us.

This is what it means TO KNOW HIM. When the Father dwells within us, we, too, can be one with Him!

When we understand this secret of indwelling, then we can see ourselves waiting at the door, watching and interceding for the younger son's return. We can run when we see the prodigal on the road, take him in our arms, smother him with kisses, offer him our best robe, and join in the celebration!

Why? Because we know the Father's heart. The Father is living in us!

Jesus, the third son who is telling this story, is the One who will meet the requirements of the Law. He will lay down His life for the younger and the older son.

Greater love has no one than this, that he lay down his life for his friends.

John 15:13

Jesus will pay the penalty (death) for sin so that both brothers might be forgiven and go free.

This is the Father's heart—to allow every man, woman, and child the opportunity to again experience an intimate relationship with Him, a relationship that was lost in the Garden of Eden when Adam sinned.

For if, by the trespass of the one man, death reigned through that one man, how much more will those who receive God's abundant provision of grace and of the gift of righteousness reign in life through the one man, Jesus Christ.

Romans 5:17

Now the choice is ours. Are we willing to come to the Father? Jesus is the Way!

Part V:
❧ Conclusion ❧

"I Love You, Bruce!"

"My son, Bruce, is very ill," said Grace, calling from the heart of Mexico where she was serving as a director of a Christian orphanage. "A bone-marrow transplant, which we felt had brought on a remission of his long-term cancer condition, only slowed the growth process of the cancer cells.

"Fred, I wish you would call Bruce. He remembers you and he needs someone to help him through this difficult time."

"When I called Bruce," said Fred, "he shared with me the serious nature of his condition. Then as we talked about old times, he asked about my family.

"'Bruce,' I said, 'I would be happy to pray and ask the Lord to heal you.'

"'Oh, I couldn't ask you to do that.'

"'Why not?' I asked.

"Bruce paused, then said: 'I'm not worthy to be prayed for.'

"I was surprised that Bruce would say that and told him so.

"'Well, Fred,' he said, 'I've wandered so far from God that praying wouldn't do any good.'

"'Bruce,' I replied, 'you cannot wander too far from God. He is your Heavenly Father—waiting, longing for you to come back to Him.'

"Days later, when I went to see Bruce at the University Hospital Cancer Center, he was on heavy medication—alert, but going in and out of sleep. Bruce's doctor came in and for almost 20 minutes shared the seriousness of his condition, saying that Bruce had only six months at the most to live.

"After the doctor left, I shared with Bruce the story of the prodigal son (Luke 15:11-32), emphasizing that even now his Heavenly Father was waiting to receive him back and longing to have a close, personal relationship with him.

"I opened the Scriptures and showed Bruce how Jesus Christ had identified with his total humanity:

For this reason he [Jesus] had to be made like his brothers in every way, in order that he might become a merciful and faithful high priest in service to God, and that he might make atonement for the sins of the people.

Hebrews 2:17

and had been tempted like Bruce *in every way.*

For we do not have a high priest who is unable to sympathize with our weaknesses, but we have one [Jesus] who has been tempted in every way, just as we are—yet was without sin.

Hebrews 4:15

"Then I showed Bruce how Jesus had taken all of his sins and transgressions upon Himself and nailed them to the cross.

When you were dead in your sins and in the uncircumcision of your sinful nature, God made you alive with Christ. He forgave us all our sins, having canceled the written code, with its regulations, that was against us and that stood opposed to us; he took it away, nailing it to the cross.

Colossians 2:13-14

"When Bruce read those verses, his face lit up and he said, 'That must include me!'

"'Yes, Bruce,' I said. 'That includes you! Let's take all that you are, all that you have done, and give it to Jesus.'

"With tears of repentance Bruce renounced his backsliding and his sins. As faith of his being accepted by the Father rose in his heart, a great big smile crossed his face. Then peace settled upon him and he fell asleep.

"In the weeks and months that followed, I visited Bruce at his home and in the hospital. As his physical condition deteriorated, his relationship with his Heavenly Father grew.

"Every once in a while Bruce would call me, sharing past sins, bondages, or broken relationships. As we prayed together, the Lord brought more and more freedom to his heart.

"Weeks later as I was talking to Pam, telling her about Bruce and his battle with cancer, God placed a burden on her heart to pray for him.

"One evening she and Jack went to see Bruce at his home.

"It was quite a shock when I saw Bruce for the first time," said Pam. "He was sitting in a recliner, drinking juice from a straw, with a pillow to support his neck. Thin, pale, and emotionally fragile, words did not come easily for him, and over the whole room there seemed to be a presence—a strong spirit of fear and death—as his mom and aunt looked on.

"I took a seat on the couch, next to the cat, telling myself I would wait for an opportunity to speak, or until the Lord specifically told me what He wanted me to do.

"Jack did all the talking. He helped Bruce forgive his dad, who years before had gone home to be with the Lord. Then he prayed that Bruce would receive the love of his Heavenly Father.

"Jack also prayed that the blood of Jesus would flow through Bruce's veins and completely heal his body. Then he encouraged Bruce to take a few steps, which he did—something he had been unable to do for weeks.

"As the days passed, I continued to pray, often with tears. Sometimes late at night or a few hours before dawn the Holy Spirit would awaken me. Then, knowing that Bruce needed prayer, I would yield myself to whatever the Spirit wanted to do through me.

"One day as I was praying, I saw Jesus carrying Bruce, like a small child of six or seven years, on His shoulder. The valley was very dark and I knew, as the words came to me from the Twenty-third Psalm, that it was the valley of the shadow of death.

"Suddenly a light broke through in the distance and I saw Jesus pick up the pace. He was headed toward, not away from, the light. It was then that I knew that I had been sent to help Bruce die.

"The second time I saw Bruce, Jack again went with me. But after Jack had shared a few verses and offered a word of prayer for Bruce's healing, it was my turn.

"Now the words began to flow—not from me, but from the One who deeply loved Bruce and had sent a special messenger to reveal that love to him.

"'Bruce,' I said, 'Father wants you to know that He loves you—that He has always loved you. Even when you rebelled and walked away from Him, He never left your side.

"'He does not love you any less when you sin. Nor does He love you any more when you are right with Him. His love is unconditional.

"'One day, as I was praying, I saw Jesus walking through a dark valley. He was carrying you on His shoulder, like a small child. It says in Psalm 23:

Yea, though I walk through the valley of the shadow of death, I will fear no evil: for thou art with me; thy rod and thy staff they comfort me.

Psalm 23:4, KJV

"'Jesus is here, Bruce. Even now He is going THROUGH that valley with you. Like a shepherd, He's carrying you on His shoulder and He's not going to leave you—not for one minute.

"'Father also wants you to know that His Word is true when it says:

There is no fear in love; but perfect love casteth out fear.

1 John 4:18a, KJV

Bathe yourself in His love, Bruce. Fill yourself up so there is absolutely no room in your body, your mind, or your heart for anything else.

"'Often we struggle for faith to claim our healing. We feel so unworthy.

"'Just rest in His love. Allow that love to push out the fear so you can hear His voice and trust in Him.

"'Romans 8:38-39 tells us that nothing, not even death, can separate us from the love of God. And in the end, it's His love—His perfect love—that makes us whole.

"'Bruce, the Lord has a special purpose for your life. You're going to do things that no one else could do!'

"'I want to do it,' said Bruce, 'whatever He wants me to do.'

"It was a sacred moment, too sacred for words. But Father was gentle, and He used me.

"As the tears began to flow down my cheeks, I turned to walk away. Then I stopped, took Bruce's hand in mine, and said, 'I'll come again.' Little did I know that it was a promise—one that Bruce would hold me to when the end came.

"About two weeks after the second visit, the Holy Spirit awakened me a few hours before dawn and led me to give Bruce a copy of *The Homecoming*. In a month or two the book would be done, ready to go to the publisher. Should I wait?

"No. I sensed an urgency within my spirit. So I ran an extra copy off on the printer at church and sent it home with his mom.

"Bruce and his aunt sat and listened as Grace read the book aloud—a few paragraphs, a story, a chapter, whatever Bruce could absorb before he would drift off to sleep.

"Bruce loved the book. Hungry for the truths it shared about the Father's love, he asked again and again that his mom read it aloud to him. In fact, before he died, they had read the book through twice, from beginning to end. Bruce's favorite story was 'I Wuv Oo!'

"The third visit was four days before Bruce went home to be with the Lord. This time Fred went with me.

"Bruce was very weak physically, but his spirit was strong. He recognized us at once and smiled.

"As Fred began to share some verses from Scripture, I sat quietly and prayed, 'Lord, what would You have me do? What would You have me say?'

"After a few minutes Fred turned to me and said, 'Pam, do you have anything you want to share?'

"I hesitated. Then my voice became soft and tender.

"'Bruce,' I said, 'your aunt told me that the Lord had given you a verse:

Father, into your hands I commit my spirit.

Luke 23:46a

That was His way of telling you that it is your choice. You can go whenever you're ready.'

"'Praise God!' said Bruce as he lifted his hands toward heaven. 'Jesus, I'm ready. You can take me anytime.'

"The radiance that came over his face caused me to pause. Never had I seen such peace, such joy.

"'And Bruce,' I continued, 'I keep seeing a picture, similar to the one in the Gospel of Luke, of the Father running to meet the prodigal.

"'I believe He's running, Bruce—even now. The Father is running to meet you and there is a celebration, a time of rejoicing that is waiting for you in glory!'

"'I'm coming! I'm coming! I'm coming!' said Bruce. 'I'm coming as fast as I can!'

"Grace nodded. My words had confirmed a picture the Lord had given her just days before.

"Then I placed my hand on Bruce's shoulder and said: 'The last thing I believe the Father wants me to tell you is that He sent me, Bruce, so that you would know how special you are to Him and how much He loves you.'

"Bruce took my hand and squeezed it tightly. With tears in his eyes, he smiled and said: 'God bless you, Pam! God bless you!'

"We shared communion with Bruce. Then we sang two of his favorite hymns, 'What a Friend We Have in Jesus' and 'Amazing Grace.'

"Bruce's eyes began to close in sleep. He was at peace.

"Three days passed and we all knew that the end was near. This time Fred went alone. Bruce's breathing was very labored and his voice so soft that even Grace was not sure at times what he was trying to say.

"'We're not going to die, Bruce. We're just going to fall asleep in Jesus and wake up in glory!'

"'Praise God!' said Bruce. 'I'm ready!'

"'You rascal! You beat me to it! You're going to see Him before I do!'

"Bruce smiled.

"'I love you, Bruce!'

"'I know you do, Fred. I love you, too. But I know that my Heavenly Father loves me even more.'

"An hour later Bruce went home to be with the Lord. He slipped away so peacefully that even the Christian nurse who was at his side did not see him go.

"But Grace did. And she sat, knowing Bruce had come full circle. From the warm, secure place in his mother's womb from which he had been born, to the 40 years he had shared with his family and friends on earth, Bruce had gone home to be with His Father in glory."

Let's not confuse religious obedience and head knowledge with relationship. It's not what we do, it's Who we know that results in eternal life! Do we KNOW Him?

Chapter Fourteen

Alive Again!

But we had to celebrate and be glad, because this brother of
yours was dead and is alive again; he was lost and is found.

Luke 15:32

Shelly, the Christian nurse, knew nothing about the words Pam had given Bruce or the illustrations that had been used in *The Homecoming.* But about an hour after Bruce went home to be with the Lord, she turned to Grace and said: "I'm seeing in the Spirit and there's a celebration going on, a party with many hugs—long hugs, happiness, and joy!"
Praise God! His love never fails.

Love never fails. But where there are prophecies, they will
cease; where there are tongues, they will be stilled; where there
is knowledge, it will pass away. For we know in part and we
prophesy in part, but when perfection comes, the imperfect dis-
appears. When I was a child, I talked like a child, I thought like
a child, I reasoned like a child. When I became a man, I put
childish ways behind me. Now we see but a poor reflection as
in a mirror; then we shall see face to face. Now I know in part;
then I shall know fully, even as I am fully known. And now
these three remain: faith, hope and love. But the greatest of
these is love.

1 Corinthians 13:8-13

When we leave this world and *"the imperfect disappears"* (v. 10) (i.e., our mortal bodies), our love for the Lord will remain. Like a legacy, it will go on before us, as our children and our children's children follow in our steps.

God's love is the bridge between life and death, the only meaning.

As a small child of six or seven, no matter how many hugs or how many kisses Grace would give him, Bruce still needed more. Love was one of his lifelong needs. He could never get enough.

But in the last eight months of his life, before his physical body succumbed to death, Bruce came to know his Heavenly Father, who is the Author of love, in a way that totally revolutionized his life and touched the lives of his immediate and extended family.

Bruce made peace with his earthly father, forgiving him for the times he had failed to meet Bruce's need for love as a child. Bruce sought reconciliation with his wife, from whom he'd been separated for a couple of years, resulting in a loving relationship that was deeper and more mature than any they had ever known.

Why? The love of God compelled him. Bruce wanted nothing to come between him and his walk with the Lord.

When the Holy Spirit would reveal sin in his life, Bruce confessed it. When he knew he was holding a grudge against someone, Bruce went to them and asked for their forgiveness.

His willingness to surrender to whatever the Lord would ask of him allowed Bruce to experience an intimate relationship with the Father. There was a dramatic change in Bruce's spirit, his countenance, and his entire physical being as I prayed for the Father to minister His healing love to him.

My wife, Dorothy, and I had known Bruce for over 30 years. In his early teens, he had accepted Jesus as His Lord and Savior. In fact, Bruce remembered that I had given him a word of prophecy that the Lord had a special purpose for his life.

A few weeks before his death, Pam would repeat these words. Little did she know that Bruce's love for the Father and his daily walk with the Lord would bring reconciliation to his family—something only Bruce could do!—as well as bring victory to many who would read the pages of this book.

We all face hardship and trials in our Christian life.

As it is written: "For your sake we face death all day long; we are considered as sheep to be slaughtered."

Romans 8:36

But like Bruce, we can be more than conquerors! How? *"Through him who loved us"* (v. 37b).

It's love that brings the victory in life and in death—the love of the Father that sent His only Son to die for us that we, though dead in our trespasses and sins, might be alive again!

> *We were therefore buried with him through baptism into death*
> *in order that, just as Christ was raised from the dead through*
> *the glory of the Father, we too may live a new life.*
>
> Romans 6:4

What can separate us from the love of God? Says the Apostle Paul:

> *For I am convinced that neither death nor life, neither angels*
> *nor demons, neither the present nor the future, nor any powers,*
> *neither height nor depth, nor anything else in all creation, will*
> *be able to separate us from the love of God that is in Christ*
> *Jesus our Lord.*
>
> Romans 8:38-39

If we have accepted Jesus as our Lord and Savior, NOTHING, not even death, can separate us from the love of God!

In life and in death, Bruce saw his Heavenly Father running to meet him!

How about us? Are we ready to meet the Father in glory? Will it be a joyous homecoming?

When we allow God's perfect love to cast out all fear, like Bruce we can say, "I'm coming! I'm coming! I'm coming! I'm coming as fast as I can!"

One group remains in Luke's parable of the prodigal: the hired servants. They are not sons, nor are they a permanent part of the family. Yet, they live on the father's estate, earning wages for their labor.

Perhaps we are serving God in full-time ministry as a priest, a rabbi, a pastor, or a missionary. Or as a layperson we are teaching a Sunday school class, leading a young people's group, serving as an usher, or singing in the church choir.

But that does not make us a son or daughter. That does not mean that we have a personal relationship with the Father.

God is our Creator, but He is not our Father until we are spiritually born into His family. Only the new birth can establish that relationship for us in heaven.

In reply Jesus declared, "I tell you the truth, no one can see the kingdom of God unless he is born again."

John 3:3

Have we experienced the second birth mentioned in John 3:1-21?

Just as Moses lifted up the snake in the desert, so the Son of Man must be lifted up, that everyone who believes in him may have eternal life. For God so loved the world that he gave his one and only Son, that whoever believes in him shall not perish but have eternal life. For God did not send his Son into the world to condemn the world, but to save the world through him.

John 3:14-17

Let's not confuse religious obedience and head knowledge with relationship. It's not what we do, it's Who we know that results in eternal life! Do we KNOW Him?

Now this is eternal life: that they may know you, the only true God, and Jesus Christ, whom you have sent.

John 17:3

The Pharisees are zealous in their devotion for God. They study the Torah; engage in long, complicated prayers; and do their best to keep His commandments.

Yet, like the older son, the Pharisees are lost in their Father's house. They are seeking to establish their own righteousness based on the Mosaic Law.

For I can testify about them [the Israelites] that they are zealous for God, but their zeal is not based on knowledge. Since they did not know the righteousness that comes from God and sought to establish their own, they did not submit to God's righteousness. Christ is the end of the law so that there may be righteousness for everyone who believes.

Romans 10:2-4

The religious leaders have religion, but not relationship. They have rules, but not the love of God. Spiritually separated from their Father, they do not know Him.

Too many of us, even professing Christians, are like the Pharisees. We are trying to establish our own righteousness through good works.

If we have accepted Jesus Christ as Lord and Savior, we are righteous. It is Jesus and His righteousness that God sees, not our righteousness, when He looks upon us.

There are three sons in this parable. One has an intimate relationship with the Father. The other two sons are lost—one in a distant country, the other in his father's house.

Where are we today? In a distant country, separated from our Father, wallowing in the mud? In our Father's house, faithfully serving Him night and day, not knowing His love for us as His son or daughter? In the field, working for wages as a hired servant? Or safe in the Father's arms?

It's not what we do, it's Who we know that makes Christianity work. If we're defeated, tired of slaving for the Master, ready to pack our bags and call it quits, we need to stop and take another look. It's relationship, KNOWING HIM, that sets us free!

That's the desire, the heart of the Father for each of us—not that we fill our heads with more knowledge or try harder to please Him, but that we allow Him to father us and change us from the inside out so that we can become like Him!

That's the revelation, the relationship that Jesus died to give us. What we lost in the Garden of Eden through sin, we can now find in redemption through the blood of Christ. Jesus is the Way to the Father!

Father loves us and we are precious in His sight. He longs to have a close relationship with each of us, but like the father in the story, He will not force Himself upon us.

Can we humble ourselves and become as a little child? Can we admit that we need Him to love us and father us as His own?

Father is standing at the door, waiting. Ready to run the minute He sees us on the road. Let's go to Him. Let's turn our steps toward home!

How Much Does Father Love Us?

I was speaking in Los Angeles to a predominantly black community. Each meeting was five hours long. They were a very hurting people.

Toward the end of the meetings I would say to them, "How much does Father love you?"

They'd say, "As much as Jesus!"

I'd say again, "How much does Father love you?"

They'd say, "As much as Jesus!" Then wave after wave of His healing love would flow over us.

I in them and you in me. May they be brought to complete unity to let the world know that you sent me and have loved them even as you have loved me.

John 17:23

How can Father love us as much as He loves Jesus? Father is no respecter of persons. If He loved the eldest Son more than He loved the brothers and sisters, He'd be a respecter of persons.

"Father," I said one day, "how can You love us as much as You love Jesus? Jesus is perfect."

He said, "I don't love Him because He's perfect. I love Him because He's My Son."

We don't have to be perfect to be loved. Father loves us because we are in Christ and we are His sons and daughters.

This is not a thought for the day. This is a thought for a lifetime.

How much does Father love us? He loves us as much as He loves Jesus!

Notes to Sources

1. Toni Auble, *My Father's Heart*. Edited version of story that appeared in the July-August-September 1993 issue of *The Message of the Cross*, a magazine published by Bethany Fellowship, 6820 Auto Club Road, Minneapolis, MN 55438. Used by permission.

2. *Just As I Am*. Music by William B. Bradbury. Lyrics by Charlotte Elliott.

3. *Into My Heart*. Music and lyrics by Harry D. Clarke. Copyright 1924. Renewal 1952 by Hope Publishing Co., Carol Stream, IL 60188. All rights reserved. Used by permission.

4. Ibid.

5. Robert Sadler with Marie Chapian, *Help Me Remember...Help Me Forget*. Minneapolis: Bethany House Publishers, 1981. (Formerly published as *The Emancipation of Robert Sadler*. Bethany Fellowship, 1975.) The true story of a slave who grew up with a love so powerful, it erased the nightmare of his past.

6. Brother Lawrence, *The Practice of the Presence of God*. Edited and paraphrased by Donald E. Demaray. Grand Rapids, MI: Baker Book House Company, 1975. In his conversations and letters Brother Lawrence (1611-1691) intimately shares his struggles to know and experience the love of God amidst the surroundings of confusion, opposition, and temptation.

About the Author

Jack Winter received a revelation of the "Father Heart of God" in 1977. Since then he has traveled to more than 30 nations, ministering to several groups including local churches, Youth With A Mission (YWAM), Teen Challenge, and Women's Aglow.

Jack graduated from St. Olaf College, Northfield, MN, in 1953 and from Bethany School of Missions, Bloomington, MN, in 1956, where he and his wife, Dorothy, served on staff for nine years.

In 1964 they founded Daystar Ministries, a network of healing communities that spanned the United States and was born out of the charismatic renewal. They have three grown children, Kris, Kari, and John, and currently reside in California.